Praise

'*Every Voice Matters* gives you the clarity and courage to participate in the conversations that shape your organisation. Raj shows that influence isn't reserved for senior leaders, it's built through everyday actions, thoughtful advocacy, and understanding what you stand for.'

— **Dr Asif Sadiq MBE**, chief inclusion officer, speaker and author of *From Intent to Impact*

'If you want to be known as a great leader, embracing Raj's ethos of Social Leadership is what you need. There are tools and frameworks that will help you to establish exactly what matters to you and how to share it effectively.'

— **Nathalie Fabre**, Head of Learning Enablement Services, Siemens Global Business Services

'Raj's vibrant personality and strong leadership immediately convinced me of the importance of making our voices heard and this is the true value Raj brings in her book: guiding readers to identify what makes their voice unique and how to express it in a meaningful and impactful way.'

— **Virginie Odinet**, Director of Internal Communications and Employer Branding, Dassault Systèmes

'This book is a remarkable blend of story, strategy and soul and the natural outcome of a life spent elevating voices. Raj transforms decades of leadership experience into an inspiring and immensely practical toolkit you will carry forward for life to change the world around you.'

— **Anette Maier**, global tax expert and lead of private tax

'With both strength and softness, Raj reaches every one of us. A powerful reminder that every voice matters – far more than we think. When our words are authentic and aligned with who we truly are, they gain meaning, value and impact. With empathy and courage, we must dare to lead our own journey and share it with the world. This book is a powerful call to action for us all!'

— **Giulia Guicciardini**, Business Senior Manager, 3DEXPERIENCE Lab

'In today's world, it's hard to break through the noise. *Every Voice Matters* is a stark reminder that your voice does matter. Or can. If you use it. If you have wanted to make an impact in a meaningful way and didn't know where to start, then this book is where Raj will show you how.'

— **Steven McAuley**, Business Psychologist and AI/ML Customer Engineering Manager, Google Cloud, EMEA North

'*Every Voice Matters* is a book about how you can make a difference in a world of distraction. It is for anyone who has the motivation to disrupt the systems of provocation and distraction which have come to dominate our discourse. Reading Raj's powerful message reminded me of the absolute necessity of thoughtful contribution to public conversation, today more than ever before.'

— **Tom Acland**, Chief Executive Officer,
Dassault Systèmes 3DEXCITE

'Everyone has a voice but finding it isn't always easy. In *Every Voice Matters,* Raj illustrates how your voice matters and provides practical steps that will enable you to step into your power and master your own story. This is a definitive guide to social leadership from someone who has walked the talk.'

— **Alan Newton**, experienced founder,
strategic consultant and executive coach

'In her book, *Every Voice Matters,* Raj convincingly shows why everyone has a message, so don't be afraid to share yours and motivate people to change themselves and the world for the better. Thanks for a valuable book!'

— **Nils Boeffel**, expert in large-scale
transformation

EVERY VOICE MATTERS

Raj Hayer

Social Leadership for Inclusive Innovation

Rethink

First published in Great Britain in 2026
by Rethink Press (www.rethinkpress.com)

In loving memory of Ashley, who believed I would write a book long before I did, and to Simone, Frank and Victoria who remain steadfast through thick and thin.

Contents

Introduction: Your Voice Matters

Every voice matters. Your voice matters. Sometimes it's hard to believe. It can feel as though our voices are drowned out by data, buried under everyone else's opinions. Over time, especially if we grow up hearing adages like 'quiet down' or 'speak when spoken to,' our voices can feel smaller and less impactful. There is pressure around how to speak up in society, how to speak up at work and, as a result, our voices can feel continually tuned out or muted amid all the noise.

This is where my Social Leadership framework comes in and is precisely why I wrote this book: to convince you that it's more urgent than ever that you speak up, and to show why every voice must be represented in the world. It's taken me over fifty years to finally have the unbridled confidence to speak up and speak out.

I have navigated various crossroads, trauma, isolation and more to get here, but I will no longer stay silent on the things that matter to me. And neither should you. You are diverse. You are different. You are unique. Your voice is unique and you have more power than you think. Every single one of us can drive change simply by participating where and how we can. How you decide to participate is up to you.

Underpinning this is Inclusive Innovation, rooted in cognitive diversity, ie all experiences, all education, all perspectives. The connection between Social Leadership and Inclusive Innovation is where the magic happens. First, understand yourself more deeply. Second, understand and accept others as they are. Third, build diverse teams and then learn to manage them to unleash cognitive diversity. Fourth, embrace ideas and work methods that accelerate Inclusive Innovation. And finally, share the journey in person and online and convince others to join you and learn from it. We cannot change the world alone; start with the individual human first, embrace diversity second and then you can truly ensure every voice is heard and valued.

But why you, and why now? Because let's face it, we're not doing so well. We seem to be regressing, with rising conflicts, rollbacks of equality laws, the closure of diversity, equity and inclusion (DEI) programmes and too many leaders driven more by power or profit than by principles. I grew up in a world that existed mainly offline, one that was sometimes kind, sometimes intolerant, sometimes accepting, but one that didn't always operate from respect and kindness. I want us to build an online and technological world that does better. I see respect and kindness as basic human rights, and as a shared responsibility we all must work towards. So instead of standing back and letting this evolution happen without us, what if we all chose to step up and speak up?

This book is for anyone who wants to influence the direction in which our society is heading. It's for you if you want to make your life better, own your worth, define your voice, share your narrative – and try to be a bloody good person while you're at it. To help you get started, I'll share my three-lever Social Leadership framework, driven by Social Representation, Social Participation and Social Responsibility, so you can lead more effectively, speak with purpose, leverage cognitive diversity and innovate for the future. Sharing our voices is not just our prerogative and our right; it's our responsibility as humans, but who says there can't be something in it for us too,

In this book I will share a few thoughts on why you matter and why your voice matters and needs to be heard, to enable and encourage you to share your voice clearly, confidently and authentically. After reading this book, you'll not only be able to state who you are and what you stand for, you'll feel confident sharing this in boardrooms, on stages, on podcasts, at networking events, even at family gatherings and parties with friends – and yes, online too. You'll gain practical tools to understand the value you can add to your own life, your community or organisation and the world.

This is not a book about personal brand – though we do touch on it – how to best use LinkedIn, or create a 'killer profile',[1] though we do discuss the importance of social media. I am not here to deep dive into peripheral topics of equality, privilege, race, technology and so on, as these require far more detailed explanations that go beyond the scope of this book and could not possibly be expanded upon adequately here. This book is about *you* and all that you are, what you stand for and the difference you can make in the world.

Over the past decade, global crises have led to profound and often devastating consequences for society. During the global Covid-19 pandemic,[2] we saw a critical mass of people laid off or furloughed, while restaurants, service businesses and startups struggled to stay afloat. During this time, many people realised that they wanted work that aligned with their values and gave them a sense of purpose, and that they needed new ways to reach people – methods of communication were being redefined in real time. Mastering LinkedIn quickly became a priority for many who didn't know where to turn or how to navigate a virtual job search or career change.

I have had a reluctant relationship with social media, but have come to recognise that it's just a platform like any other – the stage, the written word or a presentation. As I'd been using LinkedIn since shortly after its inception, I knew how to help the people who were now asking, 'How can I improve my LinkedIn profile and presence?' and 'How can I use it to find a job beyond the job postings?'

This is where my Social Leadership framework began, yet I quickly realised that I didn't want to talk about profile audits, gaining followers, becoming a thought leader or generating cold leads, primarily because I believe true leadership requires action, not just thought leadership. I wanted to encapsulate the idea of leadership as a contribution to society, aligned to one's values. And I wanted to include all voices. The true value of social media is in being able to understand what we each have to offer and then feeling confident enough to offer it.

Unfortunately, we are seeing voices being silenced through censorship, 'cancel culture',[3] unethical leadership, misuse of power and more. For example, it is widely believed that Steven Colbert's late night talk show was cancelled due to his open criticism of the sitting government.[4] The real issue is that, whether you agree with him or not, his voice matters. Only a willingness to hear dissenting views and have open discussion will allow us to understand all perspectives. When we 'cancel' one side of the conversation, we shrink our freedom of thought and drift into the dominant narrative, often without even realising it, because we've shut out opposing views. Jimmy Kimmel was next on the 'cancel' list, but this time, we saw something powerful happen. The masses rallied. They cancelled their subscriptions to popular online streaming platforms, thereby raising their voices together and voting with their wallets.[5] In real-time, the general population used capitalist tools to bring about the change they wanted to see. Kimmel was reinstated. It wasn't a fluke; it was feedback and response in action.

The Kimmel example proved a critical point: that all voices matter, and when they are aligned and coordinated, standing together, they can drive real change. I don't believe influence needs to be shouted, but every voice must be counted. Whether that voice is spoken aloud or expressed through ballots, wallets or attention, this is evidence that *every voice matters*. When it comes to power, attention is currency, but solidarity is leverage.

Everyone has a voice to share, and Social Leadership is about what you want to use your voice to speak about. It is about you, your voice, your actions, what you stand for and who and what you advocate for. How you show up is how we define the world.

The Social Leadership framework is for anyone who has felt marginalised, powerless and undervalued in their life or work. It is for anyone who wants to bring their organisation or community into the digital future. It is for anyone who has ideas and perspectives that can contribute to our collective future. It is for anyone who cares about our planet and the world we live in.

Are you unhappy with the direction that our society, our world is going in? Then it is time to speak up. By the time you finish this book, you'll feel confident that your voice needs to be heard.

This is Social Leadership at its core.

Every. Voice. Matters.

PART ONE
FINDING YOUR FREQUENCY

1
Take Me To Your Leader

It took me a long time, a lot of reading and studying and quite a few tools to understand and own the power I have and, more critically, accept what power I don't have. When I was first introduced to the concepts of the Circle of Concern and the Circle of Influence,[6] it came as quite a shock to learn how much energy and effort I had put into worrying about things I would never be able to control: the breaking news, the weather, a moody boss, office gossip – even how efficiently the local shop was run. It forced me to reexamine my life and accept that the only thing any of us has control over is ourselves: our body, mind, thoughts, feelings, actions, reactions and voice.

Take a moment to let this resonate with you.

You cannot control the weather. You cannot control your boss. You cannot control your family or friends. You can try, but you will always fail. You cannot always control what happens to you, but you can control how you react to it and what you do next. I could not control that I had a car accident and reconstructive facial surgery at nineteen, or open-heart surgery at twenty-three, but I could determine if I wanted to stay stuck in that trauma or move forward.

The question is: are you purposeful and intentional in how you think, feel, act or react? And how do you use your voice to support that?

You are the leader of your life, responsible for making decisions that align with your values and aspirations. From this point forward, when you read the words 'leader' or 'leadership' in the text, remember that I am talking about *you*. You are a leader. It's not just those in formal leadership roles; those with titles, budgets and direct reports within organisations or communities. Embracing Social Leadership means taking ownership of your life and, most importantly, understanding that you have the power to influence what happens around you. It is about determining how you can create cohesion across your personal and professional life and impact the world by addressing societal issues that matter to you, and our collective future, in the process.

Shift the script

I've delivered my Social Leadership concept to hundreds of accomplished leaders, and seen that the most common barriers to embracing our power as leaders are our own self-limiting beliefs. One leader I coached was stuck in perfectionism mode; he knew his value proposition and what he wanted to say, but agonised over every social media post until he stopped posting at all. Another could speak confidently about her work and results, but the moment I asked about her values, beliefs and desires, she physically covered her mouth, unable to answer. A third was incredibly powerful, but worried people viewed her as tough and insensitive, and within two minutes of meeting her, I saw a wonderful sense of humour that was completely suppressed at work. Social Leadership can shift this mindset. Simply defining your value proposition can be profoundly empowering and encourage you to speak up.

Since 2022, I have had the pleasure of teaching at the EU Business School in Munich, where I am happy to donate my time and help the next generation of leaders find their voice. Interestingly, the younger generations are just as concerned about using social media responsibly; they fear the same reprisals the older generations do – namely, being judged for mistakes, not being good enough or feeling drowned out in the crowd. They struggle to see how their voice can make a difference, but have big ambitions, such as entering politics or becoming influencers. When they approach me after class to say that I have encouraged them to value their own voices and use any opportunity to share their thoughts and ideas, I feel grateful to have inspired that confidence. Social Leadership can empower younger purpose-led voices to join the fray.

Another area where a shift is needed is in gender disparities. I see two clear gender patterns emerge when coaching. The men I coach want to be known for their 'soft skills', such as supporting women in leadership, being inspirational and team-oriented, and we work on how they could express those values. The women, even those in the most senior roles, still feel unseen, pressured to prove themselves or unsure how to use their voice. The men rarely feel they need to prove that they deserve to be there or to be paid well, so they can focus on how they want to be perceived. Women, meanwhile, pack their LinkedIn profiles with lists of qualifications to prove that they have earned their place and deserve respect. Social Leadership can convince you of your own power, and you can shift to using that power to be vocal about changes you want to see.

Own your voice

I wish I had been braver earlier myself. I once worked for a leader who was warm and funny outside the office but a tyrant at work, shouting and tearing strips off people in front of the whole team. It was devastating. If I had truly owned my value and my power, I might have addressed the issue sooner. Instead, I stayed another year because I needed the job, and only when I found another job did I finally quit. Social Leadership, like any leadership, is about knowing what matters to you and choosing to lead with that. It harnesses the power of influence; it enables you to align your value system with that of your organisation or community and take social responsibility for addressing societal issues. Only then do you use online media to amplify your voice so you can pull attention to things that matter to you.

We don't have to dig too deep to find a relevant example. The Black Lives Matter movement has been active since 2013, but it wasn't until one man's murder, George Floyd, was recorded on a mobile phone video recording shared on social media platforms such as X (formerly known as Twitter), that spread awareness, organised protests and mobilised support globally.[7] The hashtag #BlackLivesMatter trended worldwide, drawing attention to systemic racism, police brutality and social injustice.[8] Millions of people across the globe shared videos, articles, personal stories and calls to action, creating a powerful, unified voice demanding change.

Imagine the influence that Martin Luther King Jr could have had with today's technology and online media platforms. Even without it, on 28 August

1963, he drew a huge number of participants to Washington DC, a pivotal event in the Civil Rights Movement.[9] Invitations were communicated through organised civil rights groups, public announcements and word-of-mouth, and yet 250,000 demonstrators from various states gathered to show their support for the movement's goals, which included the passage of the Civil Rights Act, job equality and the end of race segregation in public schools. Now imagine what King might have achieved if his iconic 'I have a dream' speech had been posted online. The reach, the impact and the change he could have influenced. Social media today helps coordinate large-scale protests, facilitates discussions and influences public opinion and policy changes. It also enables activists and organisations to connect, share resources and support each other in real time. This amplification of voice has led to tangible outcomes, such as police reforms, corporate commitments to diversity and inclusion and increased support for racial justice initiatives.

Unfortunately, online platforms have also been used for negative purposes, such as manipulation, voting scandals and 'fake news'.[10] Can we do better? Of course. To make an impact beyond ourselves we can advocate for causes we care about, draw attention to injustice and work for good. Your ability to publicly support or recommend a cause, a policy, or your company's initiatives can be amplified by social media. By engaging in Social Leadership, you not only strengthen your personal and professional identity but also contribute positively.

Everyone is a leader in their own lives. We all have a voice and can align it with what matters to us. While you may know some of this already, you may still feel doubtful or stuck. Through the course of the book, you'll find your purpose *and* your voice and get unstuck. Let's start with a little self-test, where only you are the winner. These questions will help you to reflect on how you have used your voice.

EXERCISE: SELF-TEST 1

1. When was the last time you attached your voice to something you care about? (Eg volunteering for the homeless.)
2. When was the last time you raised awareness towards a cause? (Eg climate change.)
3. When did you last foster a community? (Eg an initiative at work.)
4. Have you added your voice to drive societal change in the past two years? (Eg civic participation.)

Every voice matters, but to drive impact you first need to define a value proposition, then decide your narrative and then create clear goals so you too can create a fulfilling and purposeful journey, inspiring others to join you along the way. We'll discuss that in Part Two: Your Blueprint For Social Leadership.

2
Welcome To Your Stage

Whether you realise it or not, just as you are already a leader of your own life, you already have a stage. It might be a boardroom, a project call, a WhatsApp group, a classroom, a LinkedIn post or the dinner table. Wherever you use your voice, your choices are already affecting others, and you are standing in a spotlight every time you speak. Using your stage isn't about pursuing fame or follower counts; it's about presence and responsibility.

Your stage is the space where your story, your values and your decisions meet the people around you. You don't control what opportunities you get to speak up, but you do control how you show up when they arrive. I learned to claim my stage, not because I felt ready, but because I understood what was at stake if I stayed silent.

Your story matters

In my professional life, I have had the great fortune to record a TEDx.[11] Not only does this process teach you to be succinct, but it also teaches you how to integrate seemingly opposing topics and create a connection with your audience. In my case, I was stepping in for a colleague. The topic (his topic) was artificial intelligence (AI). I struggled to see how I could connect my personal story to AI but knew I had to say yes to the opportunity. It was such a rare opportunity back then, I had to grab it and figure it out along the way. It took a few weeks of writing, rewriting and editing before I finally felt that I had landed on a story that was relevant to me, my experience and my expertise that I could record and feel proud of. 'Addicted to AI' was my unique perspective.[12]

The reason I could record it, is because I was telling my personal story. I opened up about my own medical experiences and combined this with expertise from AI use cases to discuss the possibilities of leveraging AI in healthcare. The talk was realistic and tactical, as I wanted to illustrate that we all need to engage in and discuss these complex technological topics – ie that they are relevant to all of us. Advancements in research and technology, based on data collected from millions of previous patients through medical research, saved my life. Doctors could cut me open and replace my aortic valve and keep my heart ticking because of it. AI and machine learning too are predicated on harnessing vast amounts of data. I took time to explore how our AI addiction continues to influence the technological advancements that impact our daily lives, and has even influenced this book.

You are the data

Every voice matters, because every bit of data that AI collects determines how it develops. Nowadays, you can't join any business or strategy discussion without someone talking about AI. Yet, they often miss the most crucial component of the conversation: that *we* are the input.

Is AI good or bad? That depends. It affects how we live, the way we work and how we interact with each other. It is the reason we watch what we do on Netflix, and listen to what we do on Spotify. It influences the driving routes we take, the things we buy, the news we listen to and the people we believe. *We* are the decision-makers shaping how AI develops and how it's used simply through the data we provide, how we behave and how we interact with technology every day. Everything we do, and everything we don't do, is data that feeds the model – and those models shape the world around us. The voices that are heard online will have greater influence on how AI develops and, thereby, will decide and define the future we live in. If we are the input but half of us are not actively and intentionally responding or sharing online, then AI will learn only from the part of the population that *is* present and speaking up. If we have only misinformation, bullies, negativity and discrimination on our online platforms, then that is what will drive the evolution of AI. Is that a world you want to live in? I know I don't.

Scary Smart by Mo Gawdat, ex-CEO of Google X, is an excellent overview of this issue regarding the development of AI. He illustrates that if we are not part of the conversations taking place then we are not contributing to the development of AI and thereby its impact on our world.[13] He goes into depth on AI development and how it can go one of two ways (hence the title). He even changed his own interactions on generative AI models, saying 'Please' and 'Thank you' when asking Siri or ChatGPT to complete a task, and I can understand why. If you don't say please and thank you to a person, are they likely to think well of you? Or are they going to label you as demanding, presumptuous or just plain rude? If a child sees this behaviour modelled, how are they likely to act? AI is learning from the way we speak to it too.

Unify through advocacy

The truth is, we all live in this world, and I hope we all want it to be a good world. The power to influence how

AI develops is one thing, but social advocacy is also critical. Social advocacy promotes and supports causes that address issues of inequality, injustice and discrimination. It can also encompass raising awareness of your company and you. We are all social advocates. Mobilising everyone – all living human beings in the world, all employees in an organisation – ensures all voices will have an impact. This is the goal. Our voices can be unified as we break through the noise. We have an opportunity to influence our lives, our communities, companies, brands and yes, our world. Mo Gawdat's work points towards our responsibility as human beings to be a part of the conversation. You need to ask yourself: where do you want to live? In your internal utopia, or the real-world society around you?

Below is another short quiz for illustrative purposes. Give 'yes' or 'no' answers only and you will begin to see how relevant you are to this conversation and narrative.

EXERCISE: SELF-TEST 2

1. Are you a human being?
2. Do you reside on this planet, in this world?
3. Do you live in society and interact with others?
4. Do you interact with the government? (Paying taxes and living in society counts.)
5. Do you frequent businesses? (Bricks and mortar or online.)

Did you answer yes to any of the above? If you did, that means you are already part of the journey – now it's time to own it. The only relevant question now is: are you showing up and sharing your voice when it matters? This is your world, too. It is a privilege to be a part of it – let's not take that for granted.

3
Discover Your Power

To build a company, increase profitability, stay competitive and sustain growth, you need many ingredients working together; in other words, people collaborating and aiming for the same strategic goals. If we want to win as companies of the future, then:

- Stakeholders must be taken into consideration, not just the shareholders
- Employees must have a say, not just the board members
- Consumer beliefs and values must carry weight in company decision-making

For this, we need leadership that is founded on values, a mission larger than the day-to-day, informing our direction. We, as leaders, create a portfolio of talent and then invest in that talent. An engaged diverse workforce, led by Social Leaders, serving customers globally and influencing business strategy – this is how we build success.

Leadership has evolved

In the past, thought leadership (expertise) used to be characterised by a single executive or company serving as the primary voice, relying on traditional communication channels to disseminate their insights and perspectives. This approach often involved formal speeches, published articles and media interviews, where a designated leader shared their vision and expertise with a broad audience. The focus was on positioning one individual or organisation as the definitive authority in their field, with information flowing in a largely one-way direction from the leader to the audience. This enabled a controlled message and hierarchical communication, but limited the opportunities for interactive and collaborative engagement with a wider community.

In the present, Social Leadership is about fostering shared values, ideas and practices within a global community of stakeholders. It involves engaging with and uniting individuals across various regions and cultures through a common purpose and vision.

This approach emphasises real-time communication, meeting stakeholders where they are, on social media and other online platforms, in community forums and at events. By being present and active in these venues, Social Leaders can respond quickly to their stakeholders' concerns, share updates and participate in ongoing conversations. This dynamic and interactive model encourages a more inclusive and participatory form of leadership, one founded on transparency and trust, where everyone's voice can be heard and collaborative solutions can be developed.

In the future, Social Leadership could evolve to become even more decentralised and inclusive. Advances in technology, such as AI and virtual reality, may facilitate new ways for leaders to connect with stakeholders globally. These tools could enable more immersive and interactive experiences, allowing for real-time collaboration and decision-making across diverse groups. For example, blockchain technology[14] could further democratise leadership by providing transparent and secure platforms for voting and consensus-building, ensuring that all voices are fairly represented, on decentralised protocol such as Nostr.[15] The rise of decentralised autonomous organisations (DAOs) could shift leadership from traditional hierarchies to more fluid and distributed networks, where leadership roles are shared and rotated based on expertise and community trust.

Future-ready leadership

The emphasis on sustainability and social responsibility is also likely to intensify, with leaders needing to address increasingly complex global challenges. This could lead to the development of more sophisticated metrics for measuring impact and accountability. Yet, even at the highest echelons of a company, I find executives who lack confidence in speaking about themselves and are hesitant to use their public voice to help us shape the world. While Social Leadership can help you find a new role that is more aligned with your passion, talents or interests, it can also help you to become more future-ready. What could that look like? Holding the attention of a board room and a stage. Helping you find a place where you feel valued and that you in turn are adding value. Enabling you to find connections, build an authentic network, activate action and enable real change in the world.

Cognitive diversity

Initially, even these goals felt limited to me, because if we are talking about real change, what does that look like? What does that feel like? To me it feels like cognitive diversity for Inclusive Innovation. I had been playing with the concepts of understanding intrinsic motivators for individuals and teamwork for some time. Myers-Briggs (MBTI)[16] and 16 Personalities[17] helped me to realise that needing time alone and feeling overwhelmed in social situations was not a fault, but an internal preference, and I have used this knowledge to showcase the value of personality diversity in teams. Through the Motive Structure Analysis (MSA®)[18] professional preferences are identified, revealing where energy is gained, such as a need for continuous learning or a principle-led work environment. By deepening my knowledge and understanding of motives and motivation I inadvertently began to understand my opposites as well. That we interact, communicate and make decisions… differently.

Have you ever taken time to uncover who you are? What do you value? What drives you? What do you want to do? And, ultimately, where can you add the most value?

DEI is not just equality across race, gender or LGBTQ rights; DEI involves seeking different experiences, varying cultures, unique perspectives and meeting specific needs. It is not about treating everyone the same but about understanding each other as unique individuals and treating people equitably, by recognising their differences and enabling them to speak up from a place that embraces these. These differences are what drive Inclusive Innovation. Humans are complex, and so is diversity; that's why real innovation depends on the cross-pollination of ideas and perspectives – in other words, cognitive diversity.

Do you have the makings of a Social Leader? To find out, you need to ask yourself some fundamental questions.

EXERCISE: SELF-TEST 3

1. Do you know your value system?
2. Can you define your value proposition?
3. Is it aligned with your company's culture?
4. Are you working towards a mission or goal that benefits society or the world?
5. Do you speak out on topics that matter to you?
6. Are you influencing others for good?

As Social Leadership continues to adapt to stakeholder expectations and becomes our foundational definition of leadership, the focus must remain on building genuine connections, fostering collaboration and driving positive change within a global community through Inclusive Innovation.

PART TWO

YOUR BLUEPRINT FOR SOCIAL LEADERSHIP

4

Introduction To Social Leadership

The Social Leadership framework is built on three drivers that define who you are, what you believe in and how you interact with others. Together, these drivers translate values into visible power and purposeful outcomes. They turn your story, your choices and your everyday behaviour into a clear signal of the kind of leader you choose to be.

These drivers work from inside–out. First, we need to anchor ourselves in what we believe and our personal values (representation), then think about how we show up with others through platforms and communities (participation) and then about our impact on the world and how we steward people and the planet at a systemic scale (responsibility).

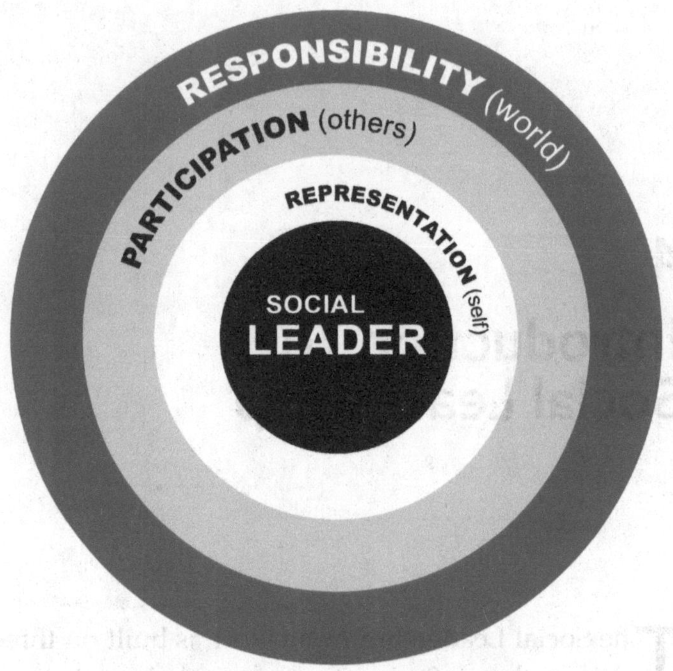

Social Leadership Framework

1. **Social Representation.** Social Leaders need to know who they are and what they believe. Social Representation is knowing what you value, your ideals, ethics, values and what you believe, and representing that. When your values align clearly with your company or community activities, this can be a real catalyst for change in the long run.
2. **Social Participation.** Social Leaders must be present and engaged in communities to have a voice. Social Participation is accepting the shift to transparency and publicity that is endemic to social media. Social Leaders understand the

power of their voice in how they, their company or community are perceived and, on a larger scale, how algorithms and AI are developed.

3. **Social Responsibility.** Social Leaders think about the bigger picture. Social Responsibility is owning what they care about, understanding the ethical impacts of what they do and the impact that their organisation has on the world. They consider the whole of society, economic growth, environmental impact and people's welfare.

By adopting these principles, you'll define your value proposition and understand on a deeper level what you want to represent and why. You will also understand that choosing not to be present is also telling a story. Social Leadership is about sharing what matters to you. It's about influencing others through your actions. You may be surprised by the power and influence you can wield. By applying these three drivers you'll see the impact of your leadership grow.

The practice of being human

What we believe in – our values – informs how we show up and speak up. It's about what we think it means to be a good human. Most successful and respected businesses wear their values proudly and have a solid framework in place – whether that's policies, procedures, guidelines or a code of conduct – to ensure consistency across the business. Being a Social

Leader is no different. If you believe there is value in Social Leadership and want 'every voice matters' to be more than a slogan, you need to start with clear rules for how you show up, speak up and treat people, online and offline.

It really is that simple – in theory, at least,

These 'Rules of Engagement' could, for all intents and purposes, be called 'How to be a good human being'. If you're part of this world, you have an obligation to be the bravest, kindest, most grounded version of yourself and, if you're intentional and a bit lucky, to leave things a little better than you found them.

This means treating everyone with respect and kindness. No one is perfect, and none of us gets it right all the time (I certainly don't), but if we start from a place of respect and kindness, we can disagree with someone's ideas while still respecting their right to have them. We can leave things and people in a better state when we pause before we react and listen before we judge. Through small, deliberate choices we can quietly improve the rooms, teams and communities we move through. These rules are not about being perfect; they're about being deliberate and using your voice in a way that makes it safer, not harder, for others to use theirs. And if all else fails, consider the sage advice: 'You'll never be criticised by someone who is doing more than you. You'll always be criticised by someone doing less.' Remember also that sometimes the most respectful response is no response at all.

Rules of Engagement for Social Leadership

Uphold the humanity of all participants. Every person in your community or organisation should be treated with respect and fairness, recognised as a human being worthy of dignity. This means valuing each person's history, contributions and perspective, regardless of background or status. When you uphold that dignity and protect the rights of others, you set a clear standard for ethical behaviour and help create a culture of safety, trust and mutual respect. Social Leadership is about building an equitable, collaborative space where diverse ideas can flourish, and everyone feels their voice is heard and, more importantly, valued.

Use language responsibly and respectfully. As a Social Leader, your words carry weight, and it's essential to use them with care. Hate speech, offensive language and inflammatory comments harm individuals and communities and erode your credibility. Social Leadership is about uniting people, seeking understanding and pushing for progress through constructive dialogue. By consciously avoiding language that provokes hostility or marginalises, you create a safe space. Leading with kindness and respect promotes a culture of inclusivity and empathy, building the trust and collaboration that will make your impact both positive and lasting.

Attack the problem, not the person. As a Social Leader, you must model behaviour that is both constructive and respectful. Avoid causing offence and harmful actions by focusing on the problem, not the person. Personal attacks and 'the blame game' damage relationships and erode the trust and cohesion needed for effective leadership. When you stick to ideas and solutions, discussions will be productive and focused on the issues at hand and moving forwards. By refraining from personal attacks, you help create and nurture an environment where differences of opinion are welcomed and you uphold the intent to understand one another and find common ground.

Engage with transparency to build trust. Transparency is the foundation of trust and meaningful connection. When you volunteer information, share sincere thoughts and genuine concerns, you give others permission to do the same. Engaging transparently and respectfully shows that you value others' opinions and experiences, even when they differ from your own. When you're open about your intentions, boundaries and perspective, you signal safety, inviting others to meet you with the same clarity, creating trust and open dialogue. Social Leadership isn't about dominating conversations or pushing a single top-down agenda; it's about facilitating inclusive, productive discussions. By embracing other people's perspectives, you broaden your own understanding and empower others to share their voices confidently – this is essential for inspiring, influencing and driving positive change in any community or organisation.

Encourage positive, constructive interactions. As a Social Leader, one of your key roles is to foster interactions that are uplifting and solution-focused. By encouraging honest and productive exchanges, you help steer conversations towards growth and collaboration. This means promoting dialogue that builds people up rather than tearing them down, and looking forwards instead of dwelling on the past. Constructive interactions strengthen relationships, increase collaboration and create a culture of learning and innovation where people feel motivated to contribute. When you lead by example, you inspire others, creating a culture of mutual respect and support that is essential for achieving shared goals.

Maintain open dialogue, reserve judgement. To ideate effectively, everyone must feel safe to share ideas and experiences. By maintaining a non-judgemental attitude and encouraging open dialogue, you foster a culture of inclusivity and mutual respect. This ensures diverse perspectives are voiced, heard and considered before conclusions are jumped to or ideas dismissed, which is essential for innovation and problem-solving. When people feel their contributions are heard rather than dismissed out of hand, they are more likely to offer new ideas and solutions. Listening without preconceived notions or bias not only strengthens relationships, but it also enhances the overall effectiveness of your team or community.

Protect the privacy and personal information of others. Safeguarding the privacy and personal information of others is a fundamental responsibility of Social Leadership. Handling sensitive details with care and never sharing information without consent builds trust and shows respect for the people you lead and work with. It also creates a safe environment where individuals feel comfortable participating without fear of exposure or misuse. By prioritising confidentiality, you nurture a culture of integrity and accountability, set a clear standard for ethical conduct and increase your credibility as a responsible and trustworthy leader.

Focus on sharing information responsibly. The information you communicate can strongly influence others, so it's essential that what you share is accurate, thoughtful and constructive. Responsible sharing means verifying facts, avoiding the spread of misinformation and considering the potential impact of your words. This helps you maintain credibility and creates an environment where trust and informed dialogue can thrive. By being mindful of the veracity of the content you share, you demonstrate integrity and set a clear standard for thoughtful, ethical knowledge sharing within your community or organisation.

Drive diversity and promote inclusivity. Promoting inclusivity means actively eliciting and valuing voices from varied backgrounds, perspectives and experiences. This enriches discussion and leads to more innovative, well-rounded outcomes. By consciously including diverse viewpoints, you ensure no one feels marginalised or overlooked, improving the quality of dialogue, products and services while building a stronger and more cohesive community. You also set a powerful example of your commitment to equality and to the belief that every person has something valuable to contribute – every voice matters.

Support a safe environment for everyone. As a Social Leader, it's your responsibility to cultivate a safe, welcoming environment based on these rules, where everyone feels safe, respected and valued. This means actively preventing harmful behaviour like bullying or harassment and addressing issues promptly when they arise. By cultivating safety, you enable people from diverse backgrounds and perspectives to participate freely and without fear. Your commitment to safety and inclusivity sets the tone for others and builds a community where everyone can engage meaningfully and contribute to collective growth.

'The Rules' may feel like a lot of information to remember, especially when you are under pressure, so start by choosing one and work towards achieving that. Then gradually, through practice, they will all become second nature and part of your everyday skill set.

Rules of engagement (at a glance)

Here's a short version of the above rules to use as a quick reference point. Return to it when conversations get heated, messy, noisy or simply for a quick check-in: *Am I showing up in a way that honours my voice and respects everyone else's?*

- Uphold the humanity of all participants
- Use language responsibly and respectfully
- Attack the problem, not the person
- Engage with transparency to build trust
- Encourage positive, constructive interactions
- Maintain open dialogue, reserve judgement
- Protect the privacy and personal information of others
- Focus on sharing information responsibly
- Drive diversity and promote inclusivity
- Support a safe environment for everyone

YOUR VOICE IN ACTION

Use these guidelines as a starting point. Add your own rules of engagement to reflect the kind of human and leader you choose to be.

5

Social Representation: Build A Foundation

The first driver of Social Leadership is Social Representation, because this is the foundation of who we are as human beings and what we want to contribute to the world. Our legacy, if you like. Social Leaders actively share their values, ideas and beliefs to influence and guide their interactions with stakeholders and communities. Values are what we regard as important, worthwhile or useful; they are our judgement of what is important in life and our standards of behaviour. I have always found that starting with my values gives me an entry point to a grander mission and vision that I want to achieve. When we establish our values, we can confidently influence for the better.

Creating influence requires leaders to be visible advocates, and to be outspoken about their beliefs.

According to the Edelman Trust Barometer 2025, leadership visibility is crucial for earning and building trust, especially in sectors like healthcare and business, and 60% of employees expect leaders to speak publicly about controversial social and political issues that matter to them.[19] Data from the 2022 barometer showed that 81% of stakeholders believe leadership should be visible at a personal level.[20]

Lead with your values

One such leader who literally put his money where his mouth was, is Dan Price, founder of Gravity Payments and CEO until 2022. Price made a bold move in 2015 that grabbed headlines and sparked conversations worldwide when he decided to raise the firm's minimum salary to $70,000. To make this happen for his 120 employees, he slashed his own $1.1 million salary.[21] So, what happened? Revenue and profit soared, and during the pandemic, the loyalty of his staff shone through as they voluntarily offered to take pay cuts to prevent layoffs.[22] Price didn't measure success just based on revenue; he looked at the real-life impact on his employees. In 2022, since implementing the salary raise, the company saw a tenfold increase in the number of first-time homeowners among its staff each year. Remarkably, 70% of his employees were able to pay down debt, with the other 30% becoming completely debt-free. They also experienced a tenfold boom in the number of babies born to employees, showing the profound personal impact of financial security. Gravity Payments' headcount doubled, and the value of payments processed by the company skyrocketed from $3.8 billion to $10.2 billion annually. They never have to post job listings because Price receives hundreds of applications per vacancy through employee referrals.[23]

Price has also become a vocal advocate on social media. He has posted on X about big companies paying executives millions in dividends or bonuses while laying off thousands of employees. He challenges companies about cost-cutting tactics, and questions why employees are let go but the executives who got them into a mess are never touched. His message has always been clear and powerful: that leaders should be held accountable, and everyone deserves a living wage – no one should live in poverty.

Price embodies Social Leadership. His actions are aligned with his values and demonstrate that taking care of employees is not just the right thing to do, it's also good for business. It can be difficult to speak up if you work for a company that would discourage this level of transparency, and you should not put yourself in a risky position. Use your discretion to determine when and how you want to speak up. The topic does not always have to be controversial – Dan Price is an extreme example. You can still find a way to speak about what you believe in and turn around a tough situation with ingenuity and authenticity.

When I was developing my Social Leadership framework, I interviewed Jürgen Schmitt,[24] who used to work on the trading desk at Deutsche Bank in Germany. Several years ago, when the bank decided to move operations to London, Schmitt's role disappeared and he was moved out of trading. Rather than seeing this as a setback, Schmitt took it as an opportunity to reflect. During a holiday shortly thereafter, he had an idea that he immediately communicated to his boss upon his return. His idea was to make short weekly videos on financial topics of interest to people both inside and outside Deutsche Bank. Schmitt's approach, which was far less corporate than traditional banks would be used to, has successfully drawn attention to the initiative and, even more crucially, the values he believes in. This innovative approach increased connectivity between different areas of the bank internally and deepened relationships with clients externally. Schmitt has no regrets about moving from trading to his new role. He has been able to influence the next generation of colleagues and make a significant impact through his creative and engaging content. His journey shows that embracing change and thinking outside the box can lead to meaningful contributions and lasting relationships within an organisation. Beyond that, he has proven that age doesn't matter when adopting new technology or trends; older generations can translate changes to new opportunities just as fast as the younger generations.

Bumble founder and CEO, Whitney Wolfe, created her business based on personal values centred on women's safety, equality and healthy relationships. She talks openly about founding Bumble 'for women to make the first move... to create a kinder, safer digital space,' and regularly shares this message via Instagram and public interviews around topics like digital safety, consent and women's empowerment. By using a social platform to advocate for her own beliefs and to amplify her company's mission in a unified, values-consistent way she has made change offline as well, helping drive Texas House Bill 2789, which made sending unsolicited explicit images a punishable offence.[25]

Giving back

Social Representation can take many forms, and my personal favourite is giving back. This is not giving back to maximise publicity for yourself, but rather because you believe in the cause itself. At TD Bank, we had a wonderful initiative that allowed us to align our personal values with meaningful community work through our partnership with Habitat for Humanity.[26] This cause was especially close to my heart because, as a teenager, I experienced poverty and homelessness. The opportunity to contribute to building homes for others resonated deeply with me on a personal level, but that's not to say I didn't have a bucketful of fun at the same time.

Participating in the Habitat for Humanity project was an incredibly fulfilling experience. It was the first time I have ever put up drywall, and while my skills in construction might not be top-notch (let's just say it's probably better for the future homeowners that I stick to painting), it was the spirit of the endeavour that mattered most. Working alongside my colleagues to build something tangible and vital for families in need brought us closer together and reinforced our shared commitment to giving back. This experience was not just about the physical act of building a home; it was about embodying the values of empathy, community and support. It taught me the importance of aligning my professional life with causes I care about and showed me the profound impact we can have when we work together as a team towards a common goal. It also meant that we were more connected through collaboration outside the workplace, got to know each other in a different environment and so deepened our personal relationships with each other.

Giving back through a company-organised activity shows a clear commitment to the cause, but of course, we can do this in our personal life too, either through a donation of funds or a donation of time. Through initiatives like these, we can make a real difference in the lives of others while also enriching our own lives and fostering a sense of purpose and connection. Social Representation therefore is about what we want to contribute to the world and what elements will guide and contribute to our Social Leadership legacy. In a way, it's simple: if you don't believe it, don't support it and don't post it.

EXERCISE: VALUES

This exercise will help you to identify what you deem worthy of your regard and what truly matters to you; this will help you narrow your focus. Your values are how you operate in the world; they are what you believe to be essential in how you live and work. They determine your priorities and your actions.

You'll need a pen and paper, or you can use the online version of my resources.

First, review Values Table A, write down the values which are important to you – at least three, no more than five. To gain insight into your authentic values, use your gut and don't overthink it.

Second, review Values Table B, identify the values which are important for you and write them down – again, you should choose at least three, no more than five, and go with your gut.

Third, transfer the values you selected from Values Table A into Values Table C for comparison.[27] Then do the same for Values Table B. See Values Table C example below.

Values Table A

Acceptance	Fairness	Originality
Accountability	Forgiveness	Professionalism
Advocacy	Fraternity	Quality
Authenticity	Freedom	Realism
Balance	Happiness/Joy	Respect/Tolerance
Bravery	Harmony	Responsibility
Charity	Honesty	Security
Clarity	Humanity	Self-determination
Collaboration	Idealism	Selflessness
Community	Inclusivity	Sincerity
Compassion	Independence	Solidarity
Competence	Initiative	Spirituality
Courage	Insightfulness	Spontaneity
Creativity	Inspiration	Support
Decisiveness	Integrity	Trust
Effectiveness	Intensity	Understanding
Efficiency	Justice	Vigour
Empathy	Kindness	Warmth
Equality	Love	Wisdom
Esteem/ Estimation	Loyalty	
	Openness	

Values Table B

Abundance
Activity
Adventure
Appreciation
Arts & Culture
Authority
Autonomy
Care/Help
Career
Challenges
Children
Communication
Contemplation
Cooperation
Cosmopolitanism
Crafts/Craftsmanship
Diversity
Education
Engagement
Environment
Eros/Sensuality
Ethics/Honour/Morals
Family

Food
Friendship
Growth
Health
High-performance
Independence
Influence
Knowledge
Leadership
Leisure/Free time
Membership/Affiliation
Money
Nutrition
Order/Structure
Ownership
Peace
Personal development
Planning
Power
Prosperity
Protection/Security
Rationality/Logic
Recognition

Relationships
Relaxation
Religion
Romance
Self-assertion
Self-criticism
Self-reflection
Serving
Silence
Sleep
Solitude
Spirituality
Sport
Stability
Status/Standing
Structure
Success
Sustainability
Tradition
Truth
Wealth
Winning
Work

Values Table C (example)

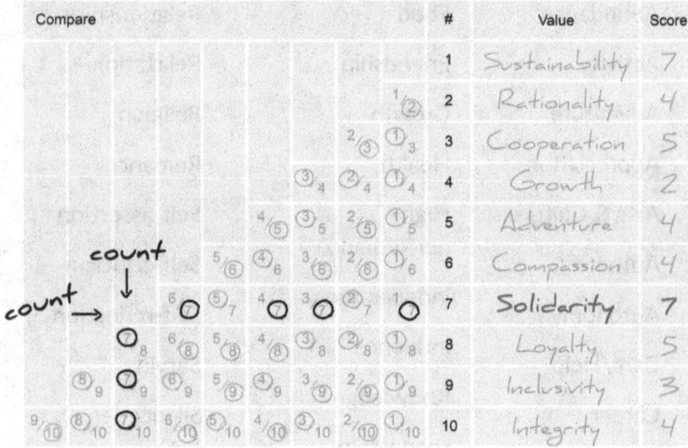

Compare	#	Value	Score
	1	Sustainability	7
	2	Rationality	4
	3	Cooperation	5
	4	Growth	2
	5	Adventure	4
	6	Compassion	4
	7	Solidarity	7
	8	Loyalty	5
	9	Inclusivity	3
	10	Integrity	4

The best way to reveal the ones that are truly important to you is through comparison and ranking. For each value you selected, take time to compare it with another and think which is the most important of the two, then circle the one that wins. Once you have completed all comparisons across all the values, you should have lots of circles. Add up all the circles for each value and write that number next to the value.

You can use the companion downloads provided for the book (see 'The Author' section for link) to conduct your values assessment or reconstruct this table.

Which values got the highest score? Take the top six from the list – these are your primary values and priorities. Write them down and keep them to hand. Now you can use these to create boundaries around your Social Leadership journey. Remember not to compromise them, offline or online.

The above exercise is a great starting point as you dig deeper into how you want to define and display your Social Leadership.

YOUR VOICE IN ACTION

Your values (Social Representation) are the foundation of who you are and how you contribute to the world. Social Leaders actively share their values and beliefs to influence and guide their interactions with all stakeholders.

6
Social Participation: Six Degrees Of Separation

Social Participation has become essential to Social Representation – in representing both yourself and the causes you care about. In the current digital age, if you are not actively part of the conversation (about you or your company), your perspective may be overlooked. That conversation is taking place without you. By being visible and engaged, you ensure that your voice is heard and that you can influence the dialogue around topics that matter to you. Active participation not only elevates your voice but also helps promote the values you believe in (Social Representation) and initiatives you support (Social Responsibility.)

Presence builds trust

Defining your voice and narrative is key to successfully navigating the online and offline landscapes. A well-defined personal brand gives you clarity about what you stand for and what you want to convey to your audience. This clarity makes it easier to share your message in a way that is both natural and effective. By consistently communicating your values and insights, you can authentically engage with your network. This authenticity helps build trust and rapport with your connections, making your interactions more meaningful and impactful.

This doesn't mean you need to limit what you support and what you care about. We are human beings, complex creatures with a multitude of interests and concerns. However, understanding your mission and defining your value proposition will make it easier to start and share, and ensure you stay aligned to the legacy you want to create. For a time, I resisted talking about women's topics because I always thought I didn't want to be perceived as someone who does not believe in equality first and foremost. Human first, diversity second is my credo. The older I get, the more I feel I need to speak about topics that matter to me, such as women and the importance of them establishing financial independence from a young age so they can create security for themselves, maximise their ability to make informed decisions and enable freedom of choice. Speaking about my values does not detract from my core topics of Social Leadership, speaking about and moderating AI and technology topics or building a community. You can still do you.

From participation to advocacy

When you have taken time to ensure your personal values resonate with your professional role, your participation on platforms like LinkedIn becomes a powerful tool for advocacy. The platforms you speak on allow you to comfortably and confidently share content that supports your company mission while also reflecting your own beliefs. This dual representation strengthens your personal brand and reinforces your company's message, creating a unified and compelling narrative that can drive engagement and build a sense of community, but only if you are participating.

LinkedIn's Chief Economic Opportunity Officer, Aneesh Raman's personal values centre on expanding economic opportunity and making the labour market fairer and more skills based. He's spent years working on this in government, tech and social-impact roles, and now writes and speaks about how AI and economic shifts are reshaping work and why opportunity needs to be more inclusive.[28] He talks about the 'bottom rung' of the career ladder breaking for young workers, why skills-first hiring matters more than pedigree and how policy, business and education can collaborate to open up opportunity. He doesn't just post to promote and market LinkedIn; he's advocating for an economic vision he clearly believes in. His values (fair access, skills-based opportunity) and his role (shaping LinkedIn's response to the future of work) reinforce each other, which is exactly the alignment you want to achieve.[29]

An example of Social Leadership in action is the Hollywood writers' strike[30] in 2023, where members of the Writers Guild of America used both in-person rallies and online platforms to advocate for protections against generative AI. By sharing personal stories, explaining how AI could undermine creative livelihoods and amplifying each other's voices on social media, writers educated the wider public about why guardrails were needed and built broad solidarity across multiple industries. This visible, values-driven advocacy helped them secure a landmark agreement that treats AI as a tool to support, not replace, writers, and guarantees credit and compensation when AI is used, showing how a united community can shape how new technologies impact work.

Company social media posts, when complemented by messages from executive leaders, make a huge difference in impact and reach. When HSBC ATMs stopped working in the UK, X was flooded with images of the screens and reactions of shock and disbelief.[31] The company immediately responded, taking to the platforms to confirm it was their mistake and that they were fixing it. Owning up to their mistake showed accountability, thereby instilling trust. What really amplified the impact, though, was the visible role of senior leaders, in this case former CEO, Noel Quinn, who was active online supporting the company's messages. Together, the official brand statements and those from its leaders reinforced the same narrative: acknowledging the issue, explaining the response and prioritising customer experience. This helped rebuild trust and demonstrated alignment in a crisis. In fact, when the CEO joined LinkedIn, he candidly admitted that social media was not his forte, which sparked a huge positive response from his employees worldwide.[32]

Join the conversation

If you are not online and responding, someone else is leading the narrative. Siemens learned this the hard way with Luo Yonghao, who famously smashed three of their refrigerators outside their Beijing offices to get their attention after they ignored his complaints about a design flaw (don't worry, he cleaned up afterwards!).[33] He had already posted a video on his blog showing the faulty door latch, repeatedly swinging it closed to prove it wouldn't catch properly. Instead of a simple, human response like 'We're sorry, thank you for flagging this, we'll fix it,' he was met with a distant answer about hiring a third party to investigate. What Siemens didn't realise was that Yonghao was highly influential and trusted for product recommendations. Within months, he was speaking for thousands of unhappy customers and directly affecting their household sales in Beijing. One thoughtful response from a single employee or leader, making customers feel heard and acknowledged, could have changed the outcome.

This kind of response from employees, leaders and companies illustrates the importance of being present and participating. Everything we do day-to-day as leaders in real life, it's possible to do online. We have moved from a single leader announcing strategy and new initiatives in a single press release, to every person in the organisation being a representative of the organisation on every social platform, in order to connect more deeply with our teams and the public. The conversation is happening with or without us, so isn't it better to be part of it?

Social Leadership means bringing your whole self to the table; not by sharing intimate details, but rather by leading with what matters to you, because what we say, what we value and how we respond matters. Knowing your value proposition makes speaking up feel natural, an authentic extension of your narrative (we'll get to this later), so you can increase your impact. This is the outcome I want for every one of you.

EXERCISE: PARTICIPATION

To be a Social Leader you need to be present both online and offline. Take time to identify the platforms where you can reach your target audience, build trust and have the most impact. At first, consider dedicating yourself to two platforms that you feel comfortable with, one online and one in person, then pick one platform where you can challenge yourself to grow as you get more confident sharing your mission and value proposition. For example, you can leverage your value proposition when speaking up in meetings and sharing on LinkedIn, and develop your proficiency and skills for public speaking by training for a TEDx.

Select two areas from the list where you already feel comfortable participating and one that you can challenge yourself in.

Participation Methods

Speaking in meetings or the boardroom

Attending conferences

Running workshops or classes

Representing communities

Speaking on stage

Guest lecturing or teaching

Volunteering for non-profits

Writing books or white papers

Appearing on podcasts

Hosting podcasts

Writing a newsletter

Contributing articles to publications

Serving on advisory councils

Participating in policy consultations

Social media	(Where is your ideal audience?)
LinkedIn:	For building credibility, leads, speaking gigs, partnerships
YouTube:	For establishing authority and search discovery
Instagram:	For visual storytelling and community warmth
TikTok:	For rapid reach with short, personality-led content
X (Twitter):	For real-time ideas, networking, distribution for links
Facebook:	For groups and local communities
Threads:	For lightweight, friendly text conversations
Substack:	For owned audience via email; long-form thinking
Medium:	For SEO-friendly essays
Pinterest:	For evergreen visual guides, checklists, lead magnets
Reddit / Quora:	For establishing authority via helpful answers
Other:	________________

Choose your platforms based on where your target audience spends time and how they prefer to consume content. Using fewer channels forces clarity; you can tailor messages to your audience and ensure you show up consistently, respond quickly and learn what works without diluting your time, energy and budget. Algorithms reward sustained, high-quality engagement and if you spread yourself too thin and across too many platforms you will not only lose energy and momentum but also weaken the power of your voice and value proposition. Three well-chosen platforms will give you enough reach, enable you to test and – most crucially – scale to reach more people, while also staying sustainable for you and valuable for your audience.

YOUR VOICE IN ACTION

Be intentional about where you represent yourself and the causes you care about. Social Leaders choose their platforms (Social Participation) with care and alignment and participate consistently to amplify their voice.

7 Social Responsibility: Choose Your Path, Use Your Power

More than a 'nice to have', Social Responsibility has become a basic customer expectation. According to the 2022 Edelman Trust Barometer, 58% of people buy or advocate for brands based on their beliefs and values, 60% choose their workplace based on these criteria and 64% invest on this basis. Even more telling, 88% of institutional investors now scrutinise ESG (environmental, social and governance) factors as rigorously as they do operational or financial reports. Societal leadership is reflecting a shift towards value-driven decision-making and is now a core business function. In an age of disruption and crisis, from the financial crash of 2008 to the global pandemic of 2020, we have survived incredible adversity that has changed us. Leadership must shift along with us – it's no longer purely about driving the bottom line; it's about aligning with values.[34]

When your values clearly align with your organisation's activities, you are a catalyst of change and can provide transparency because it's simply business as usual – you have nothing to hide. This alignment fosters trust and loyalty among stakeholders, proving that Social Responsibility and ethical decision-making are at the heart of successful and sustainable business practices.

Social Responsibility is not just a buzzword; it means being transparent about who you are, what you stand for and what matters to you, and acting accordingly. By sharing your journey, you connect with others who are looking for relatable and genuine leaders. People follow real people, not just companies, and you are one of the people they want to hear from. This is where sustainable innovation lives; this is how we can collectively impact our shared future. The more voices we have working towards the big goals, the more change we can propel and make tangible in our lifetimes and beyond.

Social Leadership embodies Social Responsibility and caring about society, including economic growth, environmental sustainability and overall welfare. This isn't just a corporate trend; it's a fundamental expectation from customers and stakeholders alike. We are moving towards a world where all stakeholders hold businesses accountable, and this accountability significantly influences customer buying decisions. We can vote for the world we want with our money in what we buy, and with our voice in what we speak up for and support. In some areas of the world, it has become the only form of vote available and remaining to populations, so let's ensure it counts.

During one of my client's events, 3DEXCITE Live, we explored the topic of sustainable consumption and the tension between fulfilling individual needs and protecting the planet, which has helped shape the concept of digital trust. Today, we can measure business activities against their environmental impact and ensure traceability across the entire lifecycle by building value networks that share and verify information.[35] This transparency is crucial for building trust, and any misleading or false ESG reporting can quickly wipe out the goodwill a brand has built online.

Purpose sparks change

Companies committed to their societal promises are started by passionate and purpose-led people. People who believe in the responsibility they have to the planet. Many people have a dream, a mission or an ultimate vision of the impact they want to make in the world. What would your mission be? What would it focus on? Environment? Sustainability? Equality? Poverty? We often think too small, staying within the frame of our own reality. When it comes to your mission in life, push yourself to dream bigger and aim higher than what seems conceivable.

Cabaïa is a French brand that sells stylish and sustainable backpacks, bags and accessories, but what you don't spot right away is that their products are made from recycled and environmentally friendly materials. Not only is Cabaïa B Corp certified,[36] they show their commitment to ethical and environmentally friendly production practices by running second-hand sales of their backpacks to encourage a circular economy, rather than one of constant replacement. They also set up the 'Care & Give' Endowment Fund[37] and a long-term partnership with Wings of the Ocean,[38] which involves active participation in waste-collection marches against wild waste and plastic pollution. They use their environment page to educate and raise awareness of environmental issues, and the role of companies in social and environmental change.[39]

Patagonia is another company that exemplifies staying true to its core values, even at the risk of reduced sales. In a now famous Black Friday ad, the brand declared 'Don't buy this jacket,' urging people not to buy for the sake of buying, but only if they had a genuine need. The message challenged consumerism, highlighted the environmental impact of overconsumption and promoted 'repair, reuse and recycle' options before buying new. We as consumers don't choose Patagonia just because we need a jacket, many brands make good ones; we choose it because of its commitment to sustainability and ethical practices. Their stance shows that business success and environmental stewardship can coexist. If this is something you care about, then find a way to share that message and use your voice to amplify this important cause.

Social entrepreneurship has grown rapidly over the past few decades, as more people build businesses or initiatives with the primary goal of creating positive social or environmental impact, while still leveraging entrepreneurial strategies to stay financially sustainable. In other words, they are using business as a tool for good. A social entrepreneur identifies a social, cultural or environmental issue – for example poverty, inequality or climate change – and develops an innovative, scalable solution with a business model that can sustain itself, rather than relying solely on donations or grants to remain purpose-led. Success, for them, is measured not just in profit, but also in impact and how much their product or service improves lives or systems. Grameen Bank's microfinance for low-income entrepreneurs is a recent example.[40] But even well-established brands have shifted towards a more values-aligned approach, such as TOMS Shoes integrating giving into its model[41] and Patagonia's focus on ensuring environmental responsibility while remaining profitable.[42] In short, a social entrepreneur blends the heart of a nonprofit with the mindset of a business leader.

Principles backed by purpose

Nike's handling of athlete Allyson Felix's return from maternity leave is a cautionary tale about public commitment to principles for any major organisation. After having her baby, Felix was offered a 70% pay cut in her role as a Nike ambassador based on the assumption that as a mother she would win less and not be as committed to her sport. Public backlash eventually pushed Nike to change its maternity-related contract policies, but the company never addressed the situation directly or apologised to Felix, missing a powerful opportunity to realign with its values and engage openly with stakeholders.[43] Felix went on to become one of the most decorated athletes in World Athletics Championship US history, holding nineteen career medals[44] and proving just how badly Nike had underestimated both her performance and the impact of her advocacy. Had Nike responded in real time, acknowledged its mistake and used its platforms to demonstrate genuine accountability and support, it could have strengthened trust; instead, its silence came across as tone-deaf, while Felix's authentic voice and story resonated far more than any delayed corporate message ever could.

Social Responsibility underscores the importance of using social platforms for sincere and honest communication. Sharing stories and passions that relate to work can help you amplify your voice and align it to causes you believe in. We all care about the world in some way, shape or form, but which topics we prioritise differ across individuals. We can't change the world by ourselves, but we can focus on bringing attention to the one topic or goal that matters most to us.

EXERCISE: MISSION

You have already identified your values; now it's time to align these with a dream that you want to see become a reality in your lifetime. Your mission statement is the inspiration for this vision and creates clarity and focus for your work. A perfect example of this is the UN's Sustainable Development goals. As explained by former UN Secretary General Kofi Annan, 'Our biggest challenge in this new century is to take an idea that seems abstract – sustainable development – and turn it into a reality for all the world's people.'[45]

If you are struggling to think big enough and need some inspiration, consider using the United Nations Sustainable Development Goals (UNSDG) below to identify the things you care about most. The UNSDG are seventeen interlinked objectives designed to serve as a shared blueprint for peace and prosperity for people and the planet.[46]

United Nations Sustainable Development Goals

1. No poverty
2. Zero hunger
3. Good health and well-being
4. Quality education
5. Gender equality
6. Clean water and sanitation
7. Affordable and clean energy
8. Decent work and economic grown
9. Industry, innovation and infrastructure
10. Reduced inequalities
11. Sustainable cities and communities
12. Responsible consumption and production
13. Climate action
14. Life below water
15. Life on land
16. Peace, justice and strong institutions
17. Partnerships for the goals

You can narrow your focus to the three that resonate most with you and where you think you can add authentic impact, or which you feel are most urgent and relevant to you personally.

Here are the three goals I am passionate about and how I contribute to them:

- **UNSDG 3: Good Health and Well-being** – I am a meditation teacher and actively support mental health initiatives such as Hope Platform[47] and Young Minds UK.[48]

- **UNSDG 4: Quality Education** – for both of my companies, core products include educational events, programmes and workshops. That's human-centred AI and cognitive diversity for TinyBox Academy,[49] and self-development tools and toolkits for Mayfly Maven.[50] I also deliver workshops at the EU Business School, on a voluntary basis.[51]
- **UNSDG 5: Gender Equality** – I campaign for, advocate for and advance women's wealth to enable freedom of choice, through hosting retreats and events such as the Wayfinders Summit,[52] featuring on the global International Women's Day Speaker List and contributing to several publications writing about the topic.

Your focus may evolve as you grow, your circumstances change and you gain new insights, but your core mission will continue to guide you. The aim is not to 'fix' the world on your own, but to keep showing up, using your skills, voice and influence in ways that move these goals forwards steadily, imperfectly and with genuine passion.

YOUR VOICE IN ACTION

Social Leadership reflects a shift towards values-driven decision-making. Social Leaders treat their chosen mission as a goal, a direction and a lifelong pursuit (Social Responsibility) rather than a short-term project.

PART THREE
STEPPING INTO YOUR POWER

8
Trust: Your Most Valuable Currency

True leadership lives or dies on trust. Whether in a relationship, a community or an organisation, trust comes through transparency. No strategy, vision or performance metric can compensate for a lack of credibility. Social Leadership is the currency of trust. I would go as far as to say that Social Leadership makes you a better person and better leader because it sharpens your ability to build trust, helping you clearly articulate your values. When you know what you stand for and can express it with confidence, speaking up – especially when you feel powerless – becomes easier, more embedded and more convincing.

When we guide others towards a shared goal in a way that feels authentic, and we prioritise transparency and trust by sharing information openly, we strengthen credibility and empower teams to perform at their best, driving innovation and success. For executives, the pressure of delivering strategy and answering to investors and boards often means they remain unaware that they are weaving a leadership story that is missing a visible, coherent leadership narrative. Moving forwards, leadership will be judged not only by financial results, but also by communication and alignment with stakeholder expectations and needs.

Become intentionally visible

Social Leadership provides the structure for alignment between internal values and external visibility, allowing you to lead with intention across all touchpoints, in person and digital, internal and external, so that executive presence becomes a strategic asset, not an afterthought. Without this, leaders risk being misunderstood, misrepresented or simply overlooked. Executives today are under increasing pressure to serve as visible role models and represent company culture, purpose and social values. Digital platforms have made leaders' decisions and actions more transparent than ever, and employees, customers and investors are no longer informed solely by company reports or press releases. They are influenced by what they hear leaders saying – or not saying – on LinkedIn, at industry events, or even in how they show up within their organisations. This is not about chasing trends or becoming a personal brand. It's about authentically and intentionally representing the values, beliefs and priorities that drive your decision-making, and doing so consistently.

Let's take my client Dassault Systèmes as an example. The company is known for leadership in 3D design and digital twin technologies, as well as a commitment to inclusive leadership. The executive team reflects a growing dedication to gender diversity, with several women in senior leadership roles across strategy, legal, research and development, operations and industry solutions. This representation is not symbolic; it reinforces Dassault Systèmes' belief that diverse perspectives drive better business outcomes and more human-centric innovation.[53]

Sharing individual leaders' stories, transparently and with intention, is essential for attracting new talent, elevating the brand and remaining competitive. People are paying attention. If a leader is not contributing to the conversation about who they are and what they stand for, others will shape their narrative for them. Executive presence must be deliberate, consistent and connected to both individual values and organisational strategy.

Finding your people

To lead today we need to be where all primary stakeholders are, and that means developing a strong online presence. Love it or hate it, you cannot avoid it. Social media has become the primary source of news, education and entertainment, revolutionising how information is consumed and shared. Platforms like X, LinkedIn, TikTok, Pinterest, YouTube, Reddit and Instagram provide real-time updates and opinions on global events, trending topics and stories, making them indispensable tools for staying informed. The immediacy and accessibility of social media enables users to engage with content, share their perspectives and connect with others worldwide, creating a dynamic and participatory media landscape that traditional outlets struggle to match. Social Leadership requires not just that you use social media, but rather that you use the *right* platforms intentionally to amplify your voice, so you can make an impact. Social media also means that it no longer matters what your title is, or indeed, if you have a 'job' at all – you can still make an impact. There have been countless examples of this in recent times.

While it was traditional media that sparked and carried the story about activist Malala Yousafzai, it was social media that amplified and sustained it to increase its impact and make it more meaningful. At just eleven years old, Malala began advocating for girls' education in Pakistan by anonymously blogging for the BBC about life under Taliban rule.[54] Her bravery brought her international attention, and after surviving an assassination attempt by the Taliban at age fourteen, she continued her advocacy with even greater resolve. Yousafzai co-founded the Malala

Fund to support education for girls globally.[55] Her platforms have enabled her to reach millions, raising awareness about the importance of education and gender equality. Her efforts have garnered substantial recognition and led to huge achievements, including receiving the Nobel Peace Prize in 2014,[56] making her the youngest laureate ever. Her story is a perfect demonstration of the powerful role digital platforms play in advocacy and social change.

Greta Thunberg also made social media platforms work for her. Thunberg, a young climate activist, began her journey by striking from school every Friday to protest climate inaction, a movement she called Fridays for Future.[57] Her solitary protests outside the Swedish parliament quickly gained international attention, largely due to her strategic use of social media platforms like X and Instagram, and she was able to mobilise millions of young people worldwide. Thirteen months after Thunberg's first protest, just before the UN Climate Action Summit started on 23 September, more than 4 million people participated in protests in 163 countries, culminating in more than 7.6 million participants in 185 countries over 8 days.[58] Thunberg's social media presence not only raised global awareness about the urgency of the climate crisis but also led to tangible actions and policy discussions. Her efforts have inspired a new generation of activists and brought climate change to the forefront of public discourse, again showing how social media can help drive significant societal change.

Crafting your narrative

Social Leadership provides a structured way to bring your values to the surface and express them in ways that resonate with stakeholders. For example, a leader who runs every morning, might do so not only for physical fitness but also so that they can run along a city's waterways to reveal its commitment to sustainability goals, looking at how the city manages and treats its water supply. Someone with a deep love of history might be guided by long-term thinking and transformation that supersedes their time in the role, thereby benefiting future generations. These are not just hobbies, they are entry points to a more relatable, meaningful leadership narrative that can be told via social media.

Once these core drivers are identified, you can map a content strategy with themes that allow you to consistently communicate who you are and how you lead. This alignment ensures that online presence, keynote speeches, town hall messages and leadership behaviours all stem from the same authentic foundation. Executives who engage with this process often experience a significant shift in how they show up, how they are perceived and how they lead. The results are measurable and meaningful:

- Stronger presence, both online and offline
- Increased trust and credibility with internal and external stakeholders

- Clearer articulation of leadership values that guide decision-making
- Greater impact in high-stakes communication, including investor calls, town halls and external speaking engagements
- Enhanced talent engagement and retention
- A leadership reputation that reflects both performance and purpose

When executives lead from a place of alignment, they create trust. They are no longer just delivering strategies; they are communicating purpose. And in a market where stakeholder trust is the currency of influence, that clarity is priceless. It doesn't happen by accident, either; it takes intentional actions, deep listening and sometimes, the disruption of old assumptions. Only then can leaders shape communication, culture, strategy and trust.

YOUR VOICE IN ACTION

You are the leader of your own life, your career and your story.

To influence impact, you need to be where your stakeholders are.

When you align your narrative to your experience, you create trust.

9
Real Transparency, Real Trust

A clear and intentional leadership narrative positions you to serve as a Social Leader, to model visibility, emotional intelligence and purpose-led communication. These qualities cascade down into teams and culture, reinforcing an organisational environment where innovation and engagement thrive. At the highest levels of business, leadership visibility is not just a communication strategy, it's a catalyst for influence, innovation and impact.

Social Leadership is about more than setting direction, it's about setting the tone. It's about aligning how you lead with how you are seen, heard and understood across all platforms and conversations. This alignment requires transparency and helps create cultural coherence, the degree to which an organisation's shared values, norms, stories and behaviours are harmonious across teams and touchpoints, creating consistent meaning and predictable action. It ensures that your voice adds value to the broader narrative of the business or community. Ultimately, it's not about having more to say, it's about saying the important things, with the right intent, in the right way and on the right platform. And that starts with knowing who you are, what you stand for and how you want to lead.

Transparency builds trust

I was working in real estate secured lending at TD Bank, one of the Big Five banks in Canada when the 2008 financial crisis hit.[59] Our employees were getting calls from panic-stricken family members and friends who were shocked by the news, and we had to navigate that as we tried to manage our own fear over our finances and potentially losing our jobs. The day after the crisis hit the news, Ed Clark, our CEO at the time, sent a message to all employees to let us know that the bank was not exposed to derivatives, but we would still be hit with the aftermath of this crisis. He then reassured everyone that no one would be laid off in the near future, to assuage the fear he knew was at the root of our discontent. However, he didn't just send an email. He spoke to his leadership teams daily and advised them to talk to their teams as information and news trickled down through the chain of command.

Everything he knew, we knew. On every floor of every office building, in every branch, the leaders would gather their teams to brief them. Our vice president would gather us together in the conference room every morning and tell us what she knew. Even if there was no new news, she would be there to answer questions as best as she could. Read that again. She would still bring us together so that she could support us and help us feel more secure, even if she had nothing new to share with us. She was visible and available to her team for questions.

When Lehman Brothers went down, shares plummeted for all banks. For TD Bank, common share price was approximately CAD$66.11 around the second quarter of 2008 and dropped by ~46.77% post-financial crisis,[60] That was when something unusual happened at our bank. Our employees started buying up shares at a reduced price. Why do you think that happened? Because they believed in the bank? Because they believed in the financial sector? (During a crisis, likely not.) Or is it more likely that they did it because they believed in our leaders?

Level up your leadership

By being transparent and bringing employees into the conversation, the leadership team at TD Bank earned a much deeper level of trust across the organisation. The impact rippled through the company culture for years. It had always been strong, but after the crisis it became impenetrable. The legendary stories about Ed Clark were widely shared, such as how he would learn all the names of the employees in the branch before visiting the frontline, or how he instilled a mentality for making process decisions – 'Would the customer pay for this?' – to ensure we were lean and always had the customer top of our minds. In fact, customers could spot a TD employee by the green pin that employees wore out and about with pride – unusual for financial services, to say the least.

During her tenure as Prime Minister of New Zealand, Jacinda Ardern demonstrated numerous powerful examples of transparency, particularly in crisis situations. She frequently hosted Facebook Live sessions, where she provided updates, answered questions and shared what she knew and what she didn't, embodying transparency and humility.[61] She built trust and ensured that the public felt informed and engaged during periods of uncertainty by giving them direct access to her. Ardern's social media presence was not just informative but empathetic. For example, her immediate and decisive response to the Christchurch Mosque shootings in March 2019 led to swift changes to New Zealand's gun laws, launching the global initiative Christchurch Call to Action to eliminate terrorist and violent extremist content online.[62, 63] By leveraging social media to maintain open and honest communication, Ardern's leadership highlighted how transparency, coupled with empathy and decisive action, could build and maintain trust domestically and internationally, even in the most challenging circumstances.

The role of transparency in building trust is even more evident today, when so much of our behaviour is visible online. But the platform for this transparency has shifted and instead of relying on meetings, town halls, newspapers, public relations and press releases, social media is the primary communication tool. This is why Social Leadership has become the new normal – when leaders are open about their decisions, challenges and vision, they create an environment where simply keeping people informed makes them feel valued. Transparency also reduces misunderstandings and hidden agendas, allowing teams to focus on shared goals. Leaders who prioritise openness can inspire loyalty and innovation while setting a standard of integrity for their organisation.

Skills over status

People management is not a superpower, but it does require skills that not everyone has or wants to develop. A title in itself shouldn't imply that someone is good at leading or is trustworthy. Unfortunately, we still often promote based on the old standard: do your job well and you'll get a promotion that comes with people management responsibilities. Yet being good at your job doesn't necessarily mean you can manage people, especially if you do not receive the requisite training. I advocate for more expert promotions, ie promotions to roles that don't include people management responsibility. Management involves taking on a huge responsibility for another person/people and their career; you must care about them, their happiness and success. Not everyone has the desire, motivation or the skills necessary to be a people manager.

Align motivation

Let's address lack of motivation first. I once ran the MSA with a manager who had been leading people for over forty years. One of the core professional parameters in the MSA is 'Lead' – in other words, are you motivated by, or do you get energy from, managing people? This is disciplinary responsibility. The opposite would be a preference to be managed and/or play an informal leadership role, such as an influencer or mentor. This manager scored 5% in this parameter. Now let me be clear, if you score low in the

Lead paradigm, this does not mean that you cannot be a great leader – you can. You can learn the skills and do it well, but you probably don't enjoy it, and it doesn't give you energy. In fact, it's likely to create a lot of stress in your life. For the leader in question, he took that information and left his people management role within three months, moving into an expert role instead. He felt much happier and was stress-free.

When we align motivators with the role, we unlock a greater sense of purpose and energy, people stay more motivated and engaged in the workplace and contribute at a higher level than those that remain unmotivated and misaligned in their roles. Make intentional job design a core part of your skills building leadership activities.

Improve skills

Now let's address lack of skills. Micromanagement is a symptom of an unskilled or untrained people manager, one who feels insecure in their role and so tries to exert control. Have you ever tried to control someone? What was the result? Children are a good example of our innate reluctance to give up control. Say 'stop fidgeting' and of course, incessant fidgeting persists. The only thing we can control and manage is ourselves, our actions and our reactions, so when someone tries to take away the little control we have, we instinctively resist it. While job design has a huge impact on employee retention and attrition, statistics show that 57% of employees have left a job because of a manager or leader.[64]

Trust goes both ways; once you have built trust with your employees, you need to trust *them* to do their work. When you try to control an employee's every activity you lose their trust. It is necessary to have oversight and involvement in your employee's work, but understanding what motivates each person is core to identifying which management style to apply. For example, I am an introvert who likes to work autonomously and independently. I like to know what I am responsible for, the results I am expected to deliver and the parameters, and then to be left to my own devices to get results. An extrovert, on the other hand, would need team interaction to keep their energy high; they like to discuss their process and get feedback before they get on with the job at hand.

Consider the impact poor leadership has on talent attraction and retention and you can imagine the knock-on effect this can have on the whole organisation. Leaders who don't understand people, often overlook the depth of the dynamics between transparency and trust. During one of my own past experiences, this became painfully evident at an all-hands meeting. The name is a nod to the maritime phrase 'all hands on deck' and implies that every crew member is pitching in; in the corporate world, it means sharing progress reports among employees. In this all-hands meeting, the leader spoke for two hours, and no employee was given time to talk. Additionally, he asked every employee, in full view of the rest of the team, to place smiley faces on a graph to indicate how happy they were in their role and with the leadership team. How many employees do you think were honest in that setting?

Shape desire

Finally, desire. If you have an exemplary employee who deserves a promotion and they want to be a people manager, then promote, train and upskill them so you can shape the kind of leader they become. Teach them how to coach, communicate and create effective team dynamics so they can succeed in the role. A leader I deeply admired, Daniele Farinaccia (alongside the dream team of people managers), once told me that his only job was 'to make sure my team is successful.' He believed that if we succeeded and wanted to work with him again, then he had succeeded as a leader. Our success reflected on him, and it's no surprise that we went on to win awards for our work.

I learned to train and manage people in my teens, working at McDonald's restaurants; their training programme for managers was comprehensive, albeit in a tough environment. However, I learned pretty fast that I don't love managing people. I prefer coaching, influencing and mentoring much more than filling out monthly performance reports or conducting yearly pay reviews. You can still add value and add to the culture of a company through an expert role, and you can still help others succeed.

Leading without managing

You don't need to be a people manager or even a formal leader to be a Social Leader. You just need to be able to motivate others. This requires being authentic to who you are, recognising what gives you energy and being capable of building trust. No one is you. No one has your unique experiences, narrative or voice to share, so be transparent and build trust as you start to amplify your voice.

Trust is built through transparency, honest interactions and genuine concern for others' well-being and growth. Ensuring that everyone involved understands the processes and reasons behind actions and your decisions helps you build trust. Social Leaders, whether they are managers or not, create an inclusive environment that encourages collaboration, empowers individuals and drives collective success. Lead with a strong sense of community and ethical responsibility and guide others by fostering open communication and sharing knowledge.

Simon Sinek said, 'People don't buy what you do, they buy why you do it.'[65] This implies that decisions are informed by emotion rather than logic. He discusses how new research into the brain's pathways has helped us understand how emotion translates into action, finding that we use emotions both as an appraisal tool and a guide for our own behaviour. This means that understanding individuals' drivers and motivations and how you can best communicate with them is a critical success factor for leading people. If you want to inspire and motivate others, if you want people to listen to or follow you, or to change their behaviour, you need to connect with what they feel and value, not just what they think.

Coca-Cola's 'Share a Coke' campaign proved this when it launched in Australia in 2011.[66] They replaced the iconic logo on bottles with 150 of the country's most popular names. This simple personalisation encouraged people to find bottles that carried their own names or those of loved ones, and share these both offline and on social media. A dedicated website and social channels helped extend the campaign's reach, and let consumers create and share virtual Coke cans, generating a wave of user-generated content. The campaign led to a 7% increase in Coca-Cola consumption in Australia, reversed a decade-long decline in sales, and was later rolled out globally with local names and cultural adaptations. This shows how a well-executed social media strategy based on understanding how people think and connecting with that, can create buzz, deepen engagement and directly influence brand perception and sales.

YOUR VOICE IN ACTION

To build trust, make sure you are transparent and visible.

Take time to develop your people management skills and exhibit humility.

To motivate others, you must understand individual drivers to gain buy-in.

10
From Stone To Ripple

A friend and I were comparing Spotify and Apple Music, on the back of the court case with Eminem and the wider discussion about the rate of pay for music artists on different streaming platforms.[67] Her argument was that this is just how the music business is built and the way the industry works. My response was, 'So what?' My reasoning was that just because the business model is predicated on not paying musicians more than they currently do, doesn't mean they can't make a change today. Sure, it was not the way business was done in the past, and it's not in the original business model, but as entrepreneurs, we learn to pivot every single day – our product, our audience, our business.

Any business can change the way it creates leaders, develops teams, represents itself and the way it operates. Organisations are full of smart people; if they wanted to, they could change things – so why not do it? Social Leadership is powered by networks that drive the adaptability and innovation we need to create ripples of change.

Network-powered ecosystems

Social Leadership and rapid technological change have shifted us from a leader-centric model to a network-powered ecosystem, where strength sits in the connections between people, teams and stakeholders. In this system, we grow, innovate and create impact together, and leadership must align with societal impact and real accountability, not just share prices. These are the growing pains of replacing a solo all-powerful executive with a values-aligned network that spans all stakeholders, built on authenticity and transparency as operating principles, not publicity campaigns. You don't just lead people; you lead signals across networks.

When decision-making is visible, trust becomes measurable, ideas flow in all directions and we can tap into collective intelligence to move faster, innovate better and embed our values into everyday practice.

A collaborative approach lets us tap into the collective strength and insight of our communities, leadership teams and employees across the organisation, creating a more dynamic and resilient system. By fostering a culture of openness and collaboration, values are not just top–down directives but are integrated into every level of our operations, becoming everyday behaviours that are visible in every role. By sharing our goals, challenges and progress transparently with stakeholders, we make decision-making more visible and understandable, so people can see the rationale behind our actions and judge how well they align with our values.

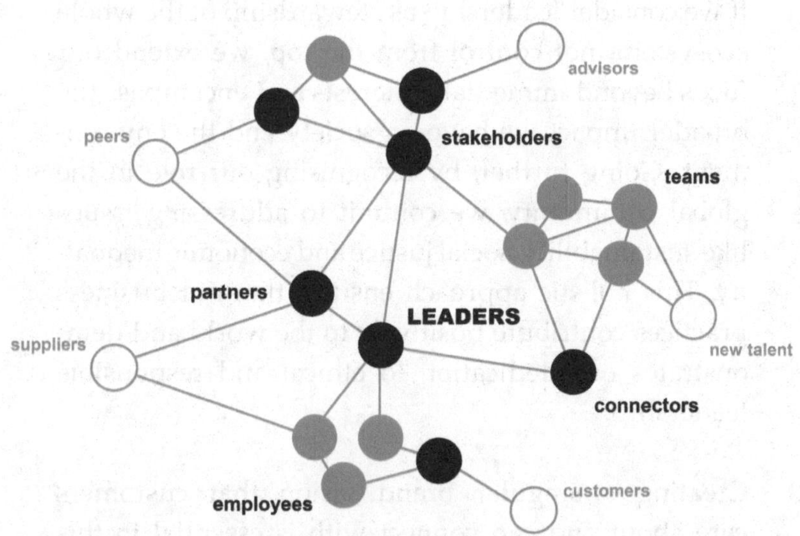

Network-powered ecosystems

This networked approach empowers every team member to contribute their unique perspective and expertise. The consequence is that innovation accelerates as ideas are freely shared and developed collaboratively, with customers becoming part of the ecosystem too. A great example of this is Adobe. The company leverages user-generated content, created with its own tools, to power Instagram campaigns like #AdobePerspective and the Art Maker Series, inviting creators to showcase how they use the software in their everyday jobs,[68] turning their community into an active, visible part of the brand.[69]

Conversations build community

If we consider leadership as stewardship of the whole ecosystem, not control from the top, we extend our focus beyond immediate interests and encompass the broader impact we have on society and the environment. Going further, by recognising our role in the global community, we commit to addressing issues like sustainability, social justice and economic inequality. This holistic approach ensures that our business practices contribute positively to the world and demonstrates our dedication to ethical and responsible leadership.

Creating a singular brand vision that customers care about and can connect with is essential in this endeavour. It's about more than just selling products or services; it's about building a brand that stands for something meaningful, and inspiring trust and loyalty among our customers. By aligning our vision with global priorities, we create a powerful connection that goes beyond transactions, demands accountability and builds lasting relationships with customers.

Showing up and being willing to have the conversation – even if it's with friends about Eminem – is crucial to achieving this vision. It means engaging openly and honestly with our customers, employees and other stakeholders about the challenges we face and the steps we are taking to overcome them. This dialogue is an opportunity to listen, learn and adapt, ensuring that our actions are informed by the needs and perspectives of those we serve. By being present and proactive in these conversations, we demonstrate our commitment to making a positive impact and invite others to join us in this journey. Together, we can create a future where business success is intertwined with the well-being of our global community.

A great example of a company in conversation with its community is LEGO. Company, employees and customers come together on the LEGO® Ideas platform. By inviting fans to submit designs for new LEGO sets and encouraging the community to vote and comment, LEGO created a collaborative space where customers help shape future products and feel like co-creators rather than just buyers.[70] Employees then review the most-supported ideas, select some for production and even credit the original fan designer. This in turn deepens engagement, builds a strong sense of belonging in the community and leads to successful commercial products that directly reflect customer creativity and feedback.

Another example is the productivity app Notion, which leans hard into community-led growth. Its ambassadors host meetups and workshops, build micro-communities, share templates and tips and get behind-the-scenes updates and support from the Notion team. These ambassadors essentially act as trusted local advocates who grow usage through education rather than ads.[71]

If you want to harness the power of community and a collective voice, creating a cohesive vision is crucial. This vision should encapsulate your core values, goals and commitments, providing a clear and compelling narrative that resonates with all stakeholders. Promoting your personal narrative within this vision is equally important. Share why this vision matters to *you*, whether it's your commitment to sustainability, your passion for innovation or your dedication to social justice. By highlighting your own motivations and experiences, you make the vision more relatable and inspiring, nurturing a deeper connection with your audience. Accelerating trustful collaboration between all relevant individuals and groups, so that stakeholders at every level – from customers and employees to partners and community members – feel seen, heard, and valued, all the while reducing negative impact on the planet, should be the goal.

YOUR VOICE IN ACTION

Adapt your leadership model to build and embrace a network-powered ecosystem.

Leverage this network to drive collaboration and innovation.

Evolve your leadership model to stewardship of the whole ecosystem.

PART FOUR
THIS IS YOUR MOMENT

11
Show Up, Stand Tall, Stay True

We all have expertise and experience that is relevant to share on various platforms. This knowledge isn't confined to your professional role; it can extend to your personal interests. By sharing your journey, you not only showcase your expertise but also motivate and guide others, embodying the true essence of leadership. Only then can you influence both brand perception and the way you personally are perceived by your peers, employees and indeed the world.

By exploring your perceptions, personal journey and professional expertise, you can define your personal brand to help you connect with others who resonate with your story. Sharing your expertise effectively through social media content will then attract followers who can benefit from your relevant experience.

Be visible and vocal

Social Leaders are accessible. What does it mean to be accessible in this world?

- To reach people, you need to be present.
- To teach people, you need to be relevant.
- To build influence, you need to be transparent.

This means that accessibility requires participation. In my executive coaching programmes, I explain that there are three core reasons and ways to participate (especially online): to inform, educate or inspire.

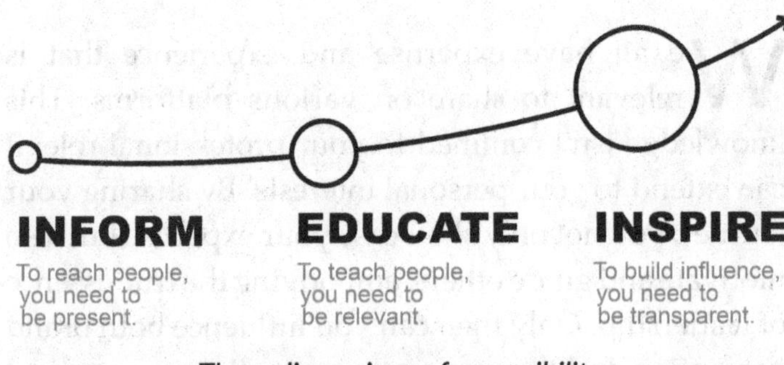

Three dimensions of accessibility

- To **inform**, share updates such as a new role, an event you're attending, an award or a milestone.
- To **educate**, share what you know, what you do, how you do it, and why it matters, drawing on your expertise and experience.

- To **inspire**, share personal stories, habits, ideas you've heard, or even your life manifesto to spark motivation in others.

Let's use an example to see how you can move from information to inspiration and make yourself accessible as a Social Leader.

You can create interest and increase brand recognition for any topic if positioned in the right way. Imagine you work at a company that offers advanced sewer inspection technology, ie vehicles for inspecting pipes, and supports the following three UNSDGs:

- UNSDG 5 Gender Equality: Make your workplace fair and inclusive
- UNSDG 6 Clean Water and Sanitation: Quality disposal and cleaning of wastewater
- UNSDG 13 Climate Action: Ethical foundation, call to action for all countries

Here is how you can connect these goals with the workplace and engage an audience online.

Inform

Create an industry-focused series of posts, but make it fun, think outside the box and connect the topic to your own experience.

When you think of the sewers, do the Teenage Ninja Turtles come to mind?

Me too. Not a surprise considering how much time I spent watching the adventures of those turtle heroes named after famous Renaissance artists.

For us at [company name], the story has a bit of a different plot…

Educate

A simple idea on how to make discussing wastewater fun is a 'Did you know...?' series that shares statistics and educates people about the sewage systems they take for granted.

Did you know [XX] tonnes of wastewater enter our oceans every day?

What can we do about it?

Well, this is what we do…

Inspire

A shout-out series is always nice to show appreciation for clients, supporters, followers, new initiatives or good deeds being done every day.

Proud of our #womeninleadership initiative here at [company name], especially [woman's name] who was just featured in [magazine] for her cutting-edge work on building sustainable water systems.

And we are just getting started.

Whenever you think of posting online, use these three words as a rule of thumb when assessing if the content is useful. Does it inform the reader, educate the reader or inspire the reader to take action? If yes, then go for it. To build trust, content must be transparent and true. Don't share content on climate action if you know you are wasteful. Don't share gender equality content if you do not have pay parity. Seems logical, right? Yet, people do it, and we see right through this inauthenticity – they immediately lose integrity and trust. Let's now take a deeper dive into the three content rules.

Inform: Give them something worth knowing

Inform your audience by sharing clear, accurate and relevant information that adds value to their understanding of a topic. Present facts, insights or updates in a way that is easily accessible and engaging, fostering informed discussions and awareness. Share relevant information in a timely fashion, including organisational or industry updates. Simply by sharing the journey of your employees you can boost employee engagement and increase talent attraction and retention. Consider posting about upcoming events you are attending, hosting or that are happening in your industry. If you are attending, then let them know where they can meet you in person – this is great for increasing client interest or expanding your network, as I experienced myself.

One of my startups was focused on people analytics and consequently, we were attending the Tucana Global Conference in London.[72] On LinkedIn, I updated my headline to say, 'Meet me at Tucana' and shared a post about the conference and who I was looking forward to listening to. About a month before the event, I took some time to research the leading minds in people analytics and key authors on the topic. I reached out to them all individually with a personalised message and asked them if they had time to meet for coffee at the festival, as I would love to discuss the topic with them. I did not know if they were attending; I did not know them through any other route or person in my network; I did not know if they would be interested or respond. And yet the result was astounding: 90% of them connected with me on LinkedIn, 44% of them replied and 2% of them were going to the conference. I was able to increase my contacts in that space in an authentic way, as I would have grabbed a coffee and been delighted to speak to them. In this way, I was able to genuinely connect with people I admire.

Another great example of engaging content that informs comes from Dropbox, a digital content-sharing and hosting platform. Dropbox uses its brand channel on LinkedIn to share informative product and company announcements while at the same time highlighting employees. Employees at Dropbox use the hashtag #LifeInsideDropbox to share stories about themselves and what they are accomplishing or doing at Dropbox. By using this hashtag, the brand account sees the content and frequently reposts and shares employee stories and content. Acknowledging employees on a public platform like LinkedIn is a great way to celebrate their successes as well as leveraging them as brand advocates. Employees are helping to motivate colleagues and shaping the future success of the organisation by influencing company culture, as well as the internal and external perceptions of Dropbox. The company not only allows them to share their journey but also supports it by sharing this organic content; in doing so, it builds a transparent and trusting work environment with a clear set of values, priorities and standards. This has had a positive impact on their employee attraction, engagement and attention, three top priorities for any organisation.[73]

By using social media to inform you can reach a particular target audience, share helpful articles, industry-related news or even marketing trends and technology advancements, thereby building trust and credibility for your organisation and you as an expert. Publish a blog post on your company or community page with a relevant or trending topic and then share it on LinkedIn for a larger reach. This can often go further than a targeted marketing campaign. By consistently sharing valuable information on LinkedIn, you can build stronger relationships with potential customers, generate leads and drive website traffic and position yourself or your company as a trusted adviser.

Educate: Turn insight into understanding

Share your expertise, your knowledge, or your experience, and teach people something they may not have known, in your own special way. Provide in-depth knowledge or skills that empower your audience to understand complex concepts or apply new learnings. Break down information into digestible, actionable insights that enhance the audience's expertise and encourage continuous learning. This is a great way to start a conversation with your customers but also a great way to find complements to your product or service so you can leverage each other's followers. Are you an accountable person who believes in a sustainable future? Then educate others on what is happening to our world. Share why it matters to you and share personal stories on why it matters and why you are focused on the topic. It's a great conversation starter and allows others to understand you and your value more deeply.

Harald Friedl is an advocate for a global circular economy, but he doesn't just talk about it, he educates others every day online and offline. Friedl educates on the circular economy by turning big-picture systems change into accessible stories, as he says 'moving from ego to eco and from intention to systemic impact.'[74] He shares his message through a practical multi-channel approach, teaching circular economy by translating systems thinking into stories, visuals and concrete use cases across several platforms. As CEO of Circle Economy, he co-initiated the Circularity Gap Report, which has become one of the most-cited global resources, shares keynotes, practical guides, white papers, coaching, programmes as well as social media and visual storytelling. Once you know what you want to share it's easy to share it through all platforms.[75]

HubSpot provides customer value on social media through content. They regularly share educational content that positions them as a trusted source of insights and trend analysis. Rather than pushing products, their approach prioritises practical knowledge that supports marketing and sales professionals in their day-to-day work. HubSpot also excels at jumping into the comments, asking open-ended questions, and turning posts into conversations, which helps build a genuine sense of community around the brand. By sharing insights openly, they share what the company cares about and can trigger conversations. The HubSpot CEO is particularly active and consistently receives thousands of reactions and responses to topics she cares about.[76]

Founder and CEO Jingjin Liu educates her audience through a mix of community-led teaching and public thought leadership. She built ZaZaZu, a corporate education platform that equips professional women with workshops and resources on professional confidence and navigating workplace challenges. She shares case studies and personal narratives on LinkedIn consistently framing confidence, inclusion and practical scripts as skills that translate from life to work.[77] When you share valuable insights, industry knowledge, or helpful tips like this, you establish yourself as an expert in your field. Educating people helps you gain visibility because it positions you as a thought leader, and sharing things you value and care about is what makes you a Social Leader.

Zoom exploded at the beginning of the global Covid pandemic, growing from 10 million daily users in December 2019 to 300 million daily users by April 2020. With so many new people on the platform, Zoom doubled down on providing tips and training through its social media networks. Helping people to become more comfortable with new products, features and services is a powerful way to use social media and show customers and clients that you have their back. Zoom did this particularly well, speaking directly to its users and showing potential customers that they prioritise client support and continuous improvement.[78]

When you use your platforms to teach, guide and support, you're not just promoting a product, you're building trust. Whether you're a product-led company or a solo expert, use the platforms available and relevant to you to walk people through new features, share how-to insights, answer common questions and demystify what you do. Educating your audience in this way turns followers into collaborators and customers into advocates. You're equipping people with knowledge, confidence and the tools to act, and that is one of the most powerful forms of influence a Social Leader can have.

Inspire: Light the spark, don't steal the fire

Motivate and uplift your audience by sharing stories, ideas or messages that spark passion and encourage positive action. This means connecting emotionally with people, helping them see new possibilities and inspiring them to pursue their goals with renewed energy and confidence. The stories you share must feel authentic and aligned with you; you can't force this – people can sense insincerity. Being authentic doesn't have to mean you have to talk about something deeply personal. Sometimes simply sharing someone else's story, and why it matters to you, can be enough to inspire.

A powerful example of inspiration at scale is the ALS Ice Bucket Challenge, launched in the summer of 2014. The campaign invited people worldwide to dump ice water on their heads, share videos on social media and donate to ALS research.[79] Whether it was empathy for those with the illness or excitement about the playful challenge of tipping a bucket of ice water over a friend, people connected with the campaign. Over 17 million people participated, including celebrities and public figures, raising $115 million globally.[80] The funds helped scientists to discover new ALS-related genes, expanded clinical trials for potential treatments and increased the number of ALS treatment centres in the US, as well as providing care services and advocacy for patients.[81] One simple, emotionally resonant idea, shared widely, turned awareness and inspiration into meaningful action.

You don't have to launch a global campaign or post details about your personal life online to inspire impact. If you choose to share something personal, make it relevant to your work and to the people you want to reach. At the Tokyo 2020 Olympics (held in 2021), Simone Biles withdrew from several events after experiencing the 'twisties' and spoke openly about prioritising her mental health over medals. Her decision was heavily debated, but it also sparked a global conversation about wellbeing in high-pressure environments. Mental health professionals and commentators note that Biles' choice encouraged not just other athletes, but all manner of people, to take their mental health seriously, set boundaries and seek help when needed, instead of pushing through at any cost.[82] She returned to the Olympics in Paris in 2024 and won gold in the individual all-around and vault, plus silver on floor and gold with the team.[83] This story shows how one person, honestly sharing a difficult decision and the reasons behind it, can give others permission to treat their own wellbeing as non-negotiable and redefine what strength looks like for them. You can inspire others who have faced the same struggles or walked a similar path by being transparent about both successes and setbacks, connecting your experiences to what you've learned and showing how they've shaped your choices.

Honest, authentic communication about your career journey, your work or the message you want to share can have a profound impact on how people see you. It strengthens your profile, deepens trust and increases the value you bring to the platform and beyond. Inspiration doesn't require a viral challenge or a perfect story; it just needs you to show up as yourself, speak from a place of truth and give others a reason to believe that their story matters too.

Start your journey

If you feel like you are ready to establish your Social Leadership presence today, then the following chapters will help you on your journey by providing a comprehensive set of resources and strategies designed to enhance your leadership capabilities in the digital age. This includes how to effectively communicate your values and ideas, engage with your audience in real time and nurture a sense of community among stakeholders. It offers insights into leveraging social media platforms, creating authentic content and using data-driven approaches to measure and improve your impact. Whether you're looking to build trust, inspire change or connect with a global network, Social Leadership equips you with the essential knowledge to lead with confidence and authenticity.

Participate with integrity

Here are three overarching guidelines, based on the themes discussed so far, to absorb before you get started:

1. **Be transparent about what you believe.** Transparency is the foundation of trust. When sharing online or in person, always be clear about your beliefs and values. Whether you're discussing industry trends, company policies or social issues, let your audience know where you stand. This openness fosters a sense of honesty and integrity, allowing others to understand your perspective and respect your authenticity. By being transparent, you create an environment where meaningful and constructive dialogue can thrive.
2. **Be authentic to who you are and your values.** Authenticity is crucial in building a genuine connection with your audience. Share your experiences, insights and opinions in a way that reflects your true self. Avoid mimicking

others or presenting a façade; instead, let your unique voice and personality shine through. Authenticity resonates with people because it's relatable and trustworthy. When you stay true to your values and principles, you inspire others to do the same and create a strong, loyal community around you.

3. **Be honest and truthful in your communication.** Honesty is essential for credibility and reliability in online interactions. Always communicate truthfully, providing accurate information as you see it or know it and acknowledging any uncertainties. Avoid exaggerations, misinformation or misleading statements, as these can damage your reputation and erode trust. When mistakes happen, own up to them and take corrective actions. Honesty not only builds trust but also encourages others to engage with you openly and respectfully, creating a culture of transparency and accountability.

YOUR VOICE IN ACTION

If your message or content informs, educates or inspires, then share it. Remember to always participate with integrity:

- Be transparent about what you believe.
- Be authentic to who you are and your values.
- Be honest and truthful in your communications.

12
Write The Story Before It Writes You

Modern communications are real-time, multi-directional and story-led. With this, you have a practical playbook to lead as a network, act as a global citizen and communicate in ways that accelerate trust and collaboration. This shift reflects the dynamic nature of today's digital world, where instant connectivity and information sharing are the norms. By communicating in real time, we stay relevant, responsive and engaged with our stakeholders, able to address their concerns and take on feedback promptly. This immediacy enhances transparency and shows our commitment to an active and ongoing dialogue. Instead of relying on one executive or one goal, we are operating and acting as part of a networked ecosystem within the global community. You must be where your stakeholders are – that means being online and engaged.

Define how you want to show up

The concept of the 'personal brand' existed long before social media; it's often overused and can mean many different things to different people. At its core, personal brand is about how you present yourself to the world, encompassing your values, skills and unique qualities. Due to its increasingly frequent use, though, the concept has become somewhat diluted and can be interpreted in various ways. For some, personal brand might mean creating a polished and professional online presence that showcases their expertise and accomplishments. For others, it could be about sharing personal stories and experiences that resonate on a more emotional level. This diversity in interpretations can make the idea of personal brand seem both expansive and vague.

Yet the essence of personal brand – being authentic and consistent in how you communicate who you are, what you stand for and what matters to you – remains important. Especially so for a Social Leader. Crucially, defining who you are and creating a personal brand *doesn't* have to involve sharing your personal life; social platforms also value educational content and honest discourse. Whether you are a professional seeking to highlight your career achievements, an entrepreneur aiming to build trust with clients or simply want to share your insights and connect with others, your personal brand reflects your identity and the value *you* bring to the table.

Bring together your values, your mission and what you care about, and you are ready to share who you are online. Understanding and embracing your personal brand means taking control of your narrative and ensuring that it represents your true self.

Find your UVP

Many of us struggle to identify the unique value proposition (UVP) and unique perspective we bring to the table – that's where finding your value proposition comes in. By exploring your past stories and experiences and reflecting on the impact you've had on others, you can begin to uncover your unique value.

During my time as an executive coach, I have come across some powerful and truly impressive men and women. Without fail, two trends emerge depending on the executive's gender. The men generally want to highlight their so-called 'soft skills' – to be known as a man who supports women, who exhibits fairness, who is a team player and who is inspirational. I can help them to define those values and share their voice. By contrast, the women often hold some of the highest positions in their companies and yet are still struggling to find their voice, feeling like they are not seen and thinking that they need to prove themselves. In these cases, the work always starts with a deeper shift in mindset before any change in actions. The men effectively got a head start – they never had to prove that they deserved to be there or to get paid a higher wage – so they can think about the other skills they want to be known for. Women, on the other hand, fill their social media profiles with lists of their qualifications as proof they have earned their positions, driven by a desire to be recognised and respected for the work they do.

I have more than once advised a woman in leadership to remove CV highlights from their social media 'about' section to personalise it and make it more about their *value*. I would say to them, 'If you have the job title you no longer need to prove you belong there – you belong there.' The people who question your place are not worth your time or energy; they are not who you are trying to engage with. One of the reasons I was motivated to write this book is that Social Leadership enables a shift in mindset that can be transformative to you and your career. Simply being able to define your value proposition beyond your basic qualifications and experience can be empowering.

Our confidence can be lifted by positive feedback or, conversely, brought down by criticism from others. In either case, it's deeply linked to our concept of our own self-worth – we are bound to what we believe about ourselves. The exercise below uses a simple but powerful process to help you own your story and define your value proposition. This isn't just a branding exercise, it's a reclaiming. A chance to shift how you see yourself, and how others see you, so you can:

- Step into any room feeling powerful and knowing what you bring to the table
- Access new opportunities and have the confidence to take them
- Have conversations with clarity and confidence in yourself

It's a self-interview process that involves understanding both how you are perceived and how you perceive yourself. The self-awareness it provides will help you identify your core skills and strengths, allowing you to define your brand more clearly and effectively highlight the unique qualities that make you stand out.

EXERCISE: STANDOUT STATEMENT

Grab a pen and paper or open a document or notes tab to get started, and set aside ten to fifteen minutes to complete this task, which involves answering a series of questions and then completing an AI-assisted task. There are no right or wrong responses, but there are a few things to remember:

- Be sure to answer the questions honestly
- Go with your gut, rapid fire is best

- Use one-word answers or short phrases (three or four words max)
- Repetition is welcome as it usually means you've hit on something core

When you're ready, start working through the four steps, which are three sets of questions/prompts followed by a task that turns your responses into your value proposition.

Step 1: Self-Perception

Use the following prompts to explore your self-perception:

- What skills do you bring to the table?
- What are you good at?
- What direct value do you provide?
- What is unique about the way you offer value?
- What personality traits do you love about yourself?
- What are your core values?
- How do you want to be described?
- How do you want to be perceived?
- If someone were asked what traits are the reason you matter, what would you hope they'd say?

Step 2: External Perception

Use the following prompts to reflect on how others see you:

- What three words would your family and friends use to describe you?
- What are three words your colleagues or peers often use to describe you?

- How would your team or partners describe your collaboration style?
- What would a satisfied client or stakeholder say you uniquely contributed to their success or experience?
- What is the one behaviour or quality that your clients rely on you for, repeatedly?
- What do your employees or peers depend on you for, especially in times of pressure?
- How about your boss or key stakeholders or investors – what do they count on you for, that others might not deliver?

If you are having trouble with this step or simply want to supercharge the process, reach out to friends and colleagues and ask them for feedback directly. I can guarantee that you'll be surprised by how willing people are to help, and you'll feel a supercharge of positive energy when you hear how they perceive you.

Step 3: Context

Before you generate your value proposition, we need to add context. So now think about:

- What is one big change or impact you want to make in the world?
- What do you care about personally or professionally?
- What are you passionate about? What is your core purpose?

Again you can use the UNSDGs as inspiration if needed.

Additionally, you need to know what audience you want to reach and how you want to impact them. This could be a specific group, a type of client or even the whole world. Ask yourself:

- Who do I want to impact?
- What influence do I want to have?
- Am I hoping to achieve a specific task, like looking for a job?

Step 4: AI Generation

Now it's time to create your value proposition. Open your preferred generative AI tool and then:

- Enter this prompt: 'Please create a one-sentence [personal/professional] value proposition based on the following: [plug in all your answers here]. Ensure it is short and succinct, and that repeated words are prioritised.'
- Copy and paste into the square brackets all your answers to the questions above.
- Click enter and watch your value proposition come to life.

Take that one sentence and examine it to see if it feels true to who you are. Maybe you need to change a word or two so that it really sounds like you. It does not need to sound fancy, but it should feel like it captures your essence.

When you've finished tweaking, congratulations – you have your value proposition.

Take a moment to reflect after completing the above exercise. How did the process feel? What surprised you? What shifted for you? Writing a value proposition is not just about finding clarity, it's about finding confidence, owning your impact and stepping forwards with intention. If you're still tweaking the sentence, that's alright. This is not about getting it perfect; it's about making the statement feel real, embodied and lived, so it resonates in how you lead, show up and serve.

Put it to work as content

Once you've refined your unique value proposition, what do you do with it? A well-defined content strategy allows you to share (Social Participation) the most relevant topics that align with your expertise, values (Social Representation) and mission (Social Responsibility). These topics serve as the foundation for your social media strategy, ensuring consistency and coherence in your messaging, whether spoken, written, visual or interactive. By homing in on key topics, you can create engaging and valuable content that resonates with your audience no matter the platform. What can you easily and wholeheartedly speak about?

Consider the following prompts and start documenting your ideas, thoughts and collecting content as you move through your days; this gives you real-life examples, use cases and stories you can share to reinforce your Social Leadership role and narrative. Here are some examples to get you started:

- What education have you completed?
- What expertise or knowledge do you have that you can share?

- What skills have you gained from experience?
- What stories do you have to share?
- Which topics are you most interested in or passionate about?
- What are your strongest opinions and viewpoints?
- What causes do you support?
- Which topics would you like to shine a light on?
- What motivates you? What do you love to do that adds value for others?
- What problem needs solving? What does the market need?

Try to include on your list the things you can speak about from the top of your head, where no research is required because you know them so well. You are more likely to speak up and share your expertise when you are interested in the topic, so don't try to create a new persona, only represent who you are. Pick two or three topics that jump out at you from your list that align with your mission, your values and value proposition, and you are ready to start participating in person or engaging online.

Once you have your topics, you can start to collect, curate and create content. This can include information, ideas and messages shared through written, visual or audible formats – any method that enables you to share it for others to consume. This content is not purely for social media but also for speaking out loud, because when you want to convince someone of your point of view, stories, examples and use cases are all highly persuasive. Your goal is to create your own portfolio or content library, so you have these resources always on hand when you need them. Many of these ideas could be applied to your internal communications strategy, as well as externally, to build trust and create engagement within your community or organisation. Your content can be converted into keynotes for the stage, an elevator pitch for conferences, anecdotes for podcasts, evidence when you are advocating for a cause or even chapters for when you write your own book.

The key to creating good content is to build a habit, keep consistent and amplify your authentic voice. When I first started posting online, I talked about leadership and coaching. Over time, I gathered those posts, spotted patterns within them and shaped them into a deeper expertise around Social Leadership, which then turned into executive coaching, courses and now this book. So, it works both ways. Sometimes we begin with a deep pool of knowledge, and your task is to break it into bite-sized, simple and digestible content for your audience. Other times you will start with those small ideas and pieces of work and eventually assemble them into something bigger, like a book or signature framework. Gary Vaynerchuk is a great example of this, he shares his ideas relentlessly across all social media platforms, then later curates and refines that same content into books. Despite the reused content, these books still sell, proving that repetition and repackaging can provide more value, not less.

A 13-week plan

Posting content is not going to immediately translate into overnight success. Mark Schaefer estimates that it takes eighteen months of consistent content creation to gain traction.[84] Mr Beast started his YouTube channel in 2012; it took him four years to reach 30,000 subscribers and he didn't go viral until 2017.[85] Focus on developing your habit, so it becomes second nature to collect, curate and create good content. Research suggests habits can take several months to stick, so give yourself at least three months or so to build the habit. Work through the examples in the plan to make content curation a habit and learn what works for you. At the same time, try to find peers in your industry and leaders and influencers in the topics you care about, while continuing your learning journey.

Week 1: Share someone else's content. If you are new to Social Leadership, this is a quick and easy method to curate content. Add your own expertise and insight to enhance the conversation. When I saw a post from an ex-colleague, it triggered me to think about how I felt working there during the financial crisis. I reposted it as an example of how integrity matters in organisations, and that how someone conducts themselves in good times directly correlates to how they act in bad times. Share advice from others, industry insights, expertise or content from a peer or an expert you respect. Notice what grabs your attention and share it with others, along with your own insights.

Week 2: Share your own content. The key to feeling confident and getting a response from your target audience is to make sure what you say aligns with your leadership narrative and content strategy. A big challenge for leadership in 2020 was how to lead employees virtually when there was no other choice, so I went back to posting about the basics – eg how to cultivate trust, motivate collaboration and make employees feel valued. (See our Rules of Engagement.) Share your expertise and insights, prepare your content in advance and, for online platforms, add a relevant image.

Week 3: Share an online article. I like to share articles that trigger a thought or reaction in me, then give my audience a link to the original so they can dive deeper. I like to use the *Harvard Business Review* and *The Economist*. Find the publications that are most relevant to your industry and content strategy and save the best pieces to share later. Remembering our rule of thumb from earlier, consider sharing a practical tip that can *inform* your audience, an insightful quote to *inspire* them or industry insights to *educate* your colleagues – anything that encourages them to click through to the article and learn more.

Week 4: Invite others to join you at an event. Are you hosting or attending an event in the coming week? Or are you or a colleague speaking anywhere? I like to support colleagues who are speaking at events and, if I am attending, I write an invitation to meet me there with a registration link or call to action included via LinkedIn, email or text. I note the main topic or industry the event is targeting and share an event highlight or a speaker that will be featured to inspire others to join me. Some events will provide attendees with 'Meet me here' social designs that you can download and use, saving you time.

Week 5: Share post-event content. I like to show respect and recognition for events as soon as possible after the event date, especially when it comes to expressing gratitude to the hosts and sharing my personal insights from the experience. What impressed you that you can share with your audience who did not get to attend? Are there any tips you took away or speakers who impressed you? Or you can simply share why someone should join or attend the next time. I save all my thoughts on my Notion app when I am at the event, adding to my library of content. A bonus idea is to host an optional lunch-and-learn session for your colleagues or peers to share your learnings from the event.

Week 6: Share a free download. Many consulting firms release a plethora of analytics and reports; find one for your industry and help others by reading it and extracting relevant content. You can share best practices, 'how to' downloads, white papers or consulting reports, but let the audience know what value they will find in the download and why they should click through.

Week 7: Share an infographic. People love infographics primarily because they allow us to take in a lot of information quickly, and they often contain extremely useful statistics, or tips and tools that can be implemented right away. If, like me, you have limited time or are not especially creative, you can find another resource to share from, just remember to credit your source. If you are handy at creating these yourself then go for it. Send them out by email to your community or colleagues or post them online.

Week 8: Write an article. Once I started writing articles, I realised how beneficial it was to my content strategy overall. One well written article is not just an article, it is a great source of multiple social media posts across different platforms; it is the inspiration for a keynote, or the invitation to a podcast interview, because the long-form format allows you to share more in-depth knowledge and expertise at a later point. If writing is a strength, this is a great way to get yourself seen and heard.

Week 9: Share an achievement or milestone. Sometimes we need to build our confidence to amplify our voice and taking a moment to recognise and celebrate our success is a great way to do this. If you don't want to toot your own horn then share how proud you are of your team, or thank people who have supported you along your journey – this is particularly powerful when landing a job or getting a book written. Share it online but also speak up at the next team meeting and say thanks.

Week 10: Share a video recommendation. Visual learning has become a preferred method of receiving information. While I still sometimes read subtitles on a video with the sound off, when I am introduced to someone new, I prefer to hear their voice so I can get to know the person and build trust. If you have watched a video that was interesting, educational or entertaining, then share it with your peers and friends. I often get video links through direct messages but do share them on social media so that your whole network can benefit.

Week 11: Record your own video. Taking to the stage and recording my keynotes has gone a long way to positioning me as an expert in my field. Recording a video is a great practice; it allows you to hear how you speak, to test your ability to share a story, learn how you convey a message and more. I prefer not to over-script so that I sound natural and tend to follow a basic structure to ensure I stay on topic and hit all the speaking points I want to deliver. You must engage your audience in the first ten seconds to convince them to keep watching. Once recorded, share your video with friends to get feedback early and, when you're ready, post it on YouTube or LinkedIn.

Week 12: Share a job posting. It is always my goal to help others succeed. It's something I learned from an old boss, and I took it to heart. Whether that is sharing a job posting, sending it to a colleague or offering introductions, I do what I can where I can. A lot of people are looking for work or transitioning in their career and sharing a job posting means that it reaches more people and more of your network. I like to pull out the main topics or skills required, and if sharing online I use keywords to make sure that the right people will see it.

Week 13: Start over and keep going. By now you have covered lots of different types of content, it's time to mix them up and continue sharing. Take the method that resonated most, that felt easier to complete, and improve on it by making it more in-depth and more relevant to your expertise or interests. Speak up and share the interesting content you've curated – online, in meetings or in your next conversation. Make sure that it aligns with your leadership narrative and content strategy, and you are good to go.

All of the above types of content sit within a powerful toolbox for success, no matter your goals. Yes, social media is the most accessible place to gain visibility and confidence, but the truth is that almost all these suggestions can be adapted to any platform you choose. If you share content thoughtfully and with intention, your brand and expertise will jump out. Whether a well-phrased post, speaking up in a meeting, or insights shared in an interview, collecting and sharing this kind of content will help you stay up to date and current in your industry, with your interests and what is happening around you.

Ultimately, be yourself. Give your expertise and knowledge away freely so your audience experiences the value you bring to the table; enable them to engage with you and it will come back to you in unexpected ways. Whether you're aiming to build a mission-led business or elevate your company's visibility, if you actively engage, you can yield significant results. Remember, the key lies in identifying your target audience and the topics that resonate with them and ensuring they align with your own interests. By consistently sharing valuable content, interacting with your community and learning from your successes, you can leverage the power of Social Leadership to propel yourself and/or your organisation towards its full potential.

YOUR VOICE IN ACTION

Follow best practices to help you maximise your impact and curate, collect and share content that is relevant to your topics. When thinking about sharing, check:

- Can you add value to the topic?
- Is it useful to your network?
- Is it going to entertain them?
- Will it give them insights into the topic?
- Will it inspire them to take action?

13
Dancing With 'What If?'

The public sphere can be intimidating, and it's natural to worry about what might happen when you step on stage, speak up in meetings or share an opinion that could trigger backlash. You have two options here.

Option one is to stay silent, not speak up and avoid social media altogether. But if you make a mistake, you lose the chance to explain, to take accountability and to shape what happens next. If you don't like the direction your team is heading, you effectively relinquish your vote. Is it better to let others have the conversation without you there to contribute, and to give up the opportunity to defend yourself?

Option two is to engage openly and trust that, when you demonstrate accountability, most people will respond with basic respect and kindness. Gaining critical feedback and opposing views builds resilience and can clarify what truly matters to you. By participating in the conversation, you have a chance to shape the narrative and show your commitment to learning and improvement.

When you make a mistake publicly, you will be held accountable, and on social media news spreads fast. A wholesome fundraiser at an elementary school turned sour when Disney fined the school $250 for showing *The Lion King* without a licence.[86] The incident quickly spread across X, causing a negative backlash for Disney. Bob Iger, Disney's executive chairman, apologised to the school on X to stem the criticism. People responded positively to his honesty and humility, appreciating that he faced the mistake head-on. While chances are you're not quite in the Disney realm yet, this example shows how being present and part of the conversation is critical to your or your organisation's reputation. So yes, speaking up is scary but what if you don't? Someone else will control the narrative, including the narrative about you.

Common fears

The most common themes that come up when clients tell me they fear public speaking or engaging with social media are:

- **Being accountable:** The fear of sharing incorrect or inappropriate content in a public domain that can lead to scrutiny, high expectations that can't be met, backlash or a damaged reputation.
- **Addressing conflict:** Concerns about getting into arguments or debates that can escalate and become public, potentially harming personal or professional relationships.
- **Facing judgement:** Anxiety about receiving negative feedback, criticism or judgement from others, for merely being who we are, and the damage this can do to self-confidence.
- **Protecting privacy:** Worries about how much to share and when it is 'too much'; the threat of personal information being exposed or misused, leading to identity theft or other security breaches.
- **Maintaining mental health:** Time consumption or addiction to being online can detract from more meaningful activities and relationships as well as impact mental health and productivity.
- **Owning unique presence:** The worry that contributions will be overlooked or deemed unimportant in the vast sea of content now at our fingertips, and feeling you have nothing special to add to the conversation.

Speaking in any public forum can indeed be daunting, but recognising these fears is the first step towards overcoming them. By addressing these concerns, you can build a more confident and mindful offline and online presence. Let's run through them one by one.

Being accountable

Speaking up on highly public forums, whether on stage or social media, means your actions and statements are on display for a wide audience. This visibility means that anything you say or post can be seen, shared and scrutinised by countless people beyond your immediate circle of friends, followers, network or audience, with potential damaging impacts if you make mistakes or express controversial opinions. A single comment, taken out of context or misinterpreted, can 'go viral',[87] attracting widespread criticism and backlash.

The worst-case scenario is that this can damage your reputation, both personally and professionally, and may lead to negative consequences such as job loss, strained relationships or potentially legal issues. Expressing controversial opinions can be particularly risky. While it's important to have open and honest discussions, social media amplifies these conversations, sometimes leading to heated debates and polarised reactions. What might be a nuanced view in a private conversation can quickly become a lightning rod for public outrage when shared online.

Being held accountable in such a public manner can also lead to being 'cancelled'. This is where individuals face severe and often disproportionate backlash for their statements or actions. This can create a climate of fear and self-censorship, where people are hesitant to share their true thoughts and opinions for fear of repercussions. You may not be able to help worrying about how you'll be perceived if you make a mistake, and how this could impact the way you are perceived by your peers. These are valid concerns.

But we all make mistakes, don't we? I don't know a single human who has not made many mistakes in their life. But mistakes are moments – they do not define you as a person. You can do a bad thing and still be a good person who did a bad thing. Will Smith slapping Chris Rock at the Oscars has been shared so often it's become a meme, and it has undoubtedly turned some die-hard fans against the actor.[88] But what is particularly relevant here is how Will Smith addressed the upset after this incident. He used his primary social media platform, Instagram, to apologise, recognising that it was the best and most direct way to reach his audience and fans.[89] The meme may live on, but if you address the issue head on, the conversation often moves on as well. It's better to face mistakes directly and engage with your audience. Yes, if you mess up, the internet knows about it instantly and one poor choice, whatever the reason for it, can, for a time, overshadow decades of work. This may make you feel tempted to avoid social media altogether, but ask yourself: is it better to let the conversation happen without you? Or is it more important to be present, transparent and build trust by taking accountability?

Turn a mistake into a win

When I worked in customer experience at a bank, we used to say that every upset customer was an opportunity to exceed expectations. The reason is that if someone is happy with your service, they tell four to six people about the experience, but if someone is unhappy with the service, upset or angry, they tell between nine and fifteen people.[90] Yet, if you listen to them, make them feel heard and rectify the situation as best you can, they aren't just happy customers, they will become your most loyal advocates.

Ryan Holmes, the CEO of Hootsuite, found himself in a social media controversy after making inappropriate comments to a journalist. Recognising the potential damage, Holmes quickly took responsibility and issued a public apology on social media, where he expressed sincere regret, acknowledged the impact and outlined steps and measures to ensure nothing like that would happen again, triggering some cultural changes at the company.[91] Social media spreads news of mistakes quickly, but it can also spread news of apologies just as fast. Holmes' quick response highlights the importance of swift and genuine apologies in handling blunders, but that can only happen if you are present and accessible. Taking responsibility, showing empathy and making concrete amends are effective strategies to maintain trust with the audience. In fact, it can enhance your integrity and credibility – and if an apology comes with action or change, as Holmes' did, it often feels more sincere.

Everyone's a critic

These days, when things go wrong with a new initiative, we find everyone online complaining about it. We can't avoid it. When the Obamacare website launched, it was burdened with many issues, and it weakened people's confidence in the healthcare programme. Reports of the issues quickly spread across social media, causing an outcry. But Obama turned the situation around by using the rather unusual comedic platform 'Between Two Ferns' where he gave a funny, humble interview with Zach Galifianakis that went viral. He admitted to the problems with the site in a witty repartee with the host, made it feel light-hearted and assured people that the healthcare programme would work. This strategic approach even reached a new younger demographic and increased website traffic by 40%. People responded positively to his honesty and humility; putting himself in the hot seat with a sharp-witted comedian who would not back down convinced many people to give the programme another chance.[92]

I realise these are big examples and big mistakes, but it works for any level of mistake. Even something as simple as misspelling a word in a post or email can create stress for people. Yet, as I point out to my clients, these small errors can endear the writer to readers because they see that not everyone is perfect. By showing your imperfections and mistakes, you allow others to feel comfortable with their own, fostering a more genuine and relatable social presence. Remember, it's OK to be imperfect; it's part of being human.

Even so, do think carefully before posting, considering how your words might be perceived and the potential impact they could have. Strive to communicate respectfully and empathetically and be prepared to take responsibility and make amends if you do cause upset or offence. By being conscious of your public presence and the power of your words, you can use any platform effectively while minimising the risk of negative consequences.

Addressing conflict

It can feel like the worst outcome when someone is argumentative, disruptive, unethical or shares a discriminatory response when you do speak up. As an introvert who deeply dislikes conflict, I find this particularly challenging. But it's important to remember that you can overcome conflict through respectful communication. Social media is meant to inspire discussion; it's a conversation, sometimes thought-provoking, and sometimes simply supportive or kind. We all have different opinions and perspectives, and we're entitled to share them.

Concerns about getting into arguments or debates that can escalate into full-blown and very public rivalries can make any environment or online platform feel unsafe. Such conflict can also become potentially harmful to personal or professional relationships, especially when they edge into the political realms, with the inevitable feeling that you must take sides. It has taken me many years to realise that one, not everything contrary requires a response, and two, that sometimes you can turn things around with a kind and understanding word. The key is to know which approach is right in a given circumstance and not be dragged into a full-blown, unproductive conflict that zaps your energy. Remember, AI algorithms will learn from how we respond to conflict, so teach it to counter hate with love and anger with patience.

Engaging in an argument is rarely productive in real life, let alone online. Instead, focus on building your tribe, your network, your friends and your audience, because they will often have your back when people do lash out, and turn it into a conversation or opportunity for learning. In 2022, Lizzo released the song 'Grrrls' with a lyric that included an ableist slur, and backlash erupted online from disability advocates and fans who explained why the word was harmful. Instead of becoming defensive or going silent, Lizzo issued a public statement acknowledging the criticism, made it clear she never wanted to use or promote derogatory language and re-recorded the track with a new lyric. She described the re-recorded song as the result of 'listening and taking action.'[93] Her response turned a heated conflict into an example of accountable communication: she listened, apologised without making excuses, corrected the harm and, in doing so, strengthened her relationship with fans and built trust with many of the people who had originally called her out.

Seek broader perspectives

It is always a comfort to find like-minded individuals and to have a community of supporters, but it's also important to stay open to new ideas, especially opposing ones, to facilitate growth and expansion beyond opinion. The first arena is representation in real life, the second is representation within an organisational culture or community and the third is fuelling that representation online. To experience this growth and expand your world, you need to be active – people need to know who you are and what you stand for. If not, you miss the opportunity for the support and connection that can enhance your work and life, and the chance to learn how to deal with conflict. We want opposing opinions and discussion to challenge us and help us grow, and we all want to be represented and feel welcome.

Social networks don't always make this easy, sometimes feeding us only more of what we like and keeping us inside a bubble. Over time this can harden opinion, amplify outrage and convince us that misinformation must be true, simply through sheer repetition. Algorithms learn our preferences and double down, reducing our exposure to cognitive diversity and weakening our ability to evaluate evidence or empathise with others. My experience of TikTok led me to jump off the platform a mere two weeks after I signed up. I watched a few X-Factor auditions (hey, the true talent shines through and I find it heartwarming to see people get a shot!) but after a few videos, that was all I was being fed on the platform, and it became extremely boring.

We as human beings are complicated, intense and deeply complex, and being reduced to just one aspect of our personality is restrictive and can make us feel like we are being imprisoned in one vein of thought. That can be suffocating. Maybe that seems dramatic, but it also feels like there is some shockingly extreme polarisation on social media platforms. Greater polarisation means faster spread of falsehoods and poorer decision-making because inputs are biased and incomplete. We hear one political ideology, one set of religious beliefs, see one audition-based show. In real life we are exposed to varying topics and ideas, and it's beneficial to have the same wide-ranged exposure online as well. I don't know about you, but I didn't study one topic in university;

I took economics, mathematics, finance and human resources, but also anthropology, psychology and even Shakespearean studies. I did this because I wanted different perspectives and a well-rounded education, learning about new and existing ideas that might influence how I saw people, business and the world. Strive to broaden your horizons and turn conflict into discussion, and you will win in the perspective you gain.

Facing judgement

Anxiety about receiving negative feedback, criticism or judgement from others can affect self-esteem and confidence, which can limit our ability to share. Everyone has an opinion, and they are not always opinions that you'll agree with. Any statement or opinion we share is out there for public scrutiny and anxiety is heightened by the fact that social media amplifies every action and reaction, exposing us to a vast audience. The fear of judgement can be paralysing, impacting our willingness to share our thoughts and engage with others. Again, it comes down to two choices: to never speak your mind, because someone somewhere will judge you for anything you say, or to realise that even your silence is judged, and you cannot avoid judgement altogether. It's the nature of the world; you can't control it. The only thing you can control is yourself, your actions and reactions. So the question is: do you feel so strongly that you are willing to put yourself on the line and stand by your beliefs and values?

Consider Emma Watson. When she delivered her HeForShe speech at the United Nations in 2014, she took a clear public stance on feminism and invited men into the conversation on gender equality. The speech went viral, but it also drew criticism from some feminists and commentators, who questioned the campaign and her role in it. In later interviews, Watson acknowledged that the backlash from people she saw as peers was difficult, but said she 'just carried on,' used some of the feedback to reflect on her approach and became more robust in the process. She continued speaking openly about feminism as freedom, liberation and equality, showing that while being judged for your opinions is inevitable, it doesn't have to stop you from engaging and advocating for what you care about.[94]

When writer Nat Eliason coined the term 'struggle porn'[95] to criticise Gary Vaynerchuk's motivational content, suggesting that he normalises sustained failure, Vaynerchuk didn't shy away from the criticism. Instead, he commented on Eliason's article, writing: 'I speak about self-awareness much more than just hustling and I agree with so much of what you're saying.'[96] His willingness to listen, reflect and engage with his critics in a constructive way, acknowledge the polarising nature of his personal brand and directly address criticism by providing context to his messaging, demonstrated a proactive approach to managing online criticism.

Being judged is inevitable, because we all have different opinions – and thank goodness, life would be boring if we all thought alike. By taking accountability and showing empathy when you are challenged or criticised, you can engage in healthy and dynamic conversations and build trust. This is your opportunity to add your voice to the throngs regardless of the backlash because every voice matters, and if we quiet our voice then the opposing side wins by default and we lose our ability to influence the society we live in. So, speak out. If there is negative feedback then put it in perspective – can you discuss this? Is your critic open to having an intelligent conversation about the topic? Then maybe there is an opportunity to have a discussion and change each other's perspective or find a middle ground.

Protecting privacy

With this specific fear, I'll focus on social media, as many individuals are concerned about privacy issues when using online platforms, worried that their personal information might be exposed or misused, or fearful of identity theft. These are legitimate concerns in our digitally connected world. Yet simply having a mobile phone means that someone, somewhere, likely already knows a lot about you, your browsing habits, your location and more. Given this reality, joining the conversation on social media might not seem like such a stretch.

We live in a society where we are exposing ourselves to similar risks every time we step out the front door. For example, a friend of mine was recently asked for money and when she said no, the person said, 'well I will just take it' and proceeded to place his mobile against her handbag, presumably to scan her card. Yes, this happens. Luckily, she had taken precautions – her Apple Tag started to beep, and she had a Magati wallet that had NFC / RFID blockers to protect against this method of theft.[97] Protecting your privacy online is a valid concern, but fear should not be the reason you don't participate, rather take measures as my friend did to protect yourself. Two-factor authentication is one of the simplest and most effective ways to protect your online accounts. It adds a second step to the login process, usually in the form of a code sent to your phone or generated by an authentication app, so even if someone manages to steal your password, they still can't access your accounts. Staying offline does not protect you from any technology-related risk, as my friend found, but there are measures you can take to protect yourself.

An example of thoughtful online privacy in practice comes from Catherine Price, a health and science journalist and author of *How to Break Up With Your Phone*.[98] She has built a strong online presence around digital wellbeing while sharing very little about her private life. Instead of posting intimate personal details, precise locations or family information, she focuses on practical, evidence-based advice to help people create healthier relationships with technology. Her work shows that you can use social media to inform, support and build a community without compromising your boundaries. By choosing what to keep offline and being intentional about what she shares, she models a balanced approach to visibility and privacy that many professionals can emulate.

If you choose to be stealthy on social media because you don't want people to know certain things about you, that's understandable. Social media is a powerful tool enabling you to engage in important conversations, to share educational content and to contribute meaningfully to discussions. Living fully in today's world means joining the conversation; whether by liking, commenting or posting, you can participate without compromising your privacy if you take extra precautions.

Maintaining mental health

Maintaining balance and protecting our mental health in real life starts with how we manage our energy, attention and relationships offline: getting enough rest, moving our bodies, setting boundaries at work and making time for people and activities that genuinely nourish us. When we protect this as the foundation of our mental health, we are better equipped to handle stress, uncertainty and the inevitable ups and downs of everyday life. Yet even with the best intentions, it's increasingly difficult to preserve this balance in a world that constantly competes for our attention. One of the most powerful forces disrupting that balance today is the pull of social media.

Social media can be a significant drain on our time and attention, with constant connectivity and instant gratification leading to excessive use of technology. With endless scrolling, notifications and a constant influx of new content, it's easy to lose track of how long we've been online, and our mental health can suffer as a result. These platforms are specifically designed to keep us engaged, with features like infinite scroll, autoplay videos, continuous notifications and algorithm-driven content tailored to our interests so that it's hard to disconnect. The urge to check for updates can disrupt our focus and reduce our efficiency, making it difficult to complete tasks or conduct deep, uninterrupted work. Beyond the obvious distraction, excessive time on social media takes us away from more fulfilling activities such as spending quality time with family and friends, pursuing hobbies or investing in our personal and professional development. Face-to-face interactions often decrease as people prioritise virtual over real-life interactions and friends. Over time, this shift can weaken our ability to build personal relationships, have meaningful conversations and maintain genuine emotional connections with others.

Prolonged exposure to curated content – the best moments of people's lives, glamorous vacations, career achievements and perfect relationships – can lead to feelings of inadequacy, anxiety and depression. We start comparing our everyday reality to the seemingly perfect lives we see online, and that comparison can leave us feeling 'not enough', isolated and less inclined to seek out meaningful, real-world interactions. The psychological impact of the discontent this breeds can be profound. Back in 2017, a study by the Royal Society for Public Health in the UK found that Instagram was associated with higher levels of anxiety, depression and loneliness, linked in part to the platform's focus on highly curated, idealised images of people's bodies and lifestyles, which fuel unhealthy comparison and feelings of inadequacy.[99] Now, these effects are only likely to become more magnified with the advent of AI image and video curation.

Seeing others' idealised lifestyles and careers can make us feel as though we are falling short, even when we are doing well by many standards. Social media algorithms tend to exaggerate this by feeding us more of the same types of posts, which can skew our perception and make it seem like everyone else is perpetually successful and happy, making us feel alone in our own struggles and ordinary moments that don't measure up. To protect your mental health, limit exposure to accounts that trigger negative comparisons and instead follow people who feel real, share authentic parts of themselves and inspire you. Take a more balanced and realistic view of both your life and the lives of others, so you can avoid comparison and preserve your self-esteem.

To further mitigate the potential for harm, it's also essential to set healthy boundaries and practise mindful social media use. This might mean setting specific times for checking your accounts, turning off unnecessary notifications and actively prioritising real-life interactions. It's OK to take a break from social media, or from technology altogether, and step back when you need to. By taking a balanced approach, you can enjoy the benefits of social media without compromising your mental health. When you consciously manage your usage, you reclaim time and energy for the activities and relationships that genuinely enrich your life.

Followers aren't the full story

The metrics associated with social media create a temptation to compete, which can negatively impact our mental health if we link our 'success' on social media to our self-worth. While consistent participation can build trust, influence and even bring in clients, chasing numbers for their own sake won't sustain you. Metrics like reactions, shares and follower counts are, at best, rough indicators, but do not define success. They can be bought, inflated or completely disconnected from real impact. A polished profile or big numbers might look impressive, but they don't necessarily imply meaningful engagement or drive the outcomes you care about. I've seen an 'influencer' with over 200,000 followers have less real impact than someone with 2,000 followers speaking from the heart and sharing relevant, honest content. One of my own posts trended with 160,000 views and 347 reactions – but not a single person contacted me or joined my network. Another post 'underperformed' with around 200 views and three reactions, yet two people reached out to work with me. They never reacted publicly; they simply saw it, sent a direct message and one of them became a client for several years. That's the difference between vanity metrics and real results. Do not let these numbers influence your behaviour or define your value.

Consistency wins over numbers, both off- and online. Showing up regularly so that your name is remembered in meetings and recognised in feeds reminds people you exist and that you have something to say. Social Leadership is about presence, not perfection. When you show up consistently, you often become more attuned to your own needs, passions and purpose, and you may even decide that you don't want to be on social media at all. The point is to participate with intention, to know yourself and to *choose* how you want to show up, rather than be driven by a pursuit of numbers that can leave you questioning your worth.

Owning unique presence

You may worry that your contributions will be overlooked or deemed unimportant, whether you're speaking on stage, sharing in a meeting or posting into the vast sea of online content. Hasn't it all been said before? What new information can you possibly add to the conversation? It's true that there is an unprecedented amount of information being shared, especially on social media. Recent estimates suggest that X users send around 500 million posts per day, almost 6,000 every second.[100] TikTok creators upload more than 23 million videos each day (around 16,000 per minute, roughly 270 per second),[101] and Instagram users share an estimated 1.3 billion images daily.[102] Combined, the major social platforms see hundreds of millions of new posts, images, videos and comments every day. Yes, it is overwhelming and it can be difficult to see the story through the noise. Yet someone, somewhere is waiting for you to share your voice.

When Amardeep Parmar finally published his first proper article on Medium in 2020, he 'didn't think anyone would care' and would have been happy if a hundred people read it. Instead, that first piece went viral, attracting over 100,000 views and earning him more than $2,000. It became the catalyst for a writing career that led to tens of thousands of followers and a complete transformation of his professional life.[103] His story shows that what feels 'obvious' to you or has 'already been said' can still be exactly what some people need to hear. Your words, at that moment, still have value to someone. Everyone has something to share, and even if a point has been made before, it becomes unique when it comes from you, alongside your perspective and insights. You are not competing with the noise; you are simply adding your voice to the collective conversation. The message may not seem new at first, but on closer examination there are always nuances in how each of us sees things, what we feel about situations and how we express ourselves.

Also, repetition isn't necessarily redundant. Consider two software engineers sharing similar contributions, both are experts in software development and share content on social media. Engineer A is a first-generation immigrant mother leading a payments team at a telehealth startup; she posts about patient safety, on-call fatigue during her child's pneumonia and the ethics of charging device failures. Engineer B works at a fast-paced trading company. He talks about how he is making their software run faster, cutting tiny delays about reducing memory slowdowns, and shares a story about how he trimmed a few millionths of a second from a critical task. They're talking about the same topic – software development – but the people who will find their content *meaningful* and *useful* are unlikely to be the same. One speaks to founders, product leaders, caregivers and regulated industries who see reliability as care. The other will resonate with die-hard finance engineers, and a systems-interested audience in pursuit of speed. Despite having similar expertise and covering similar topics, they will attract different audiences with their unique perspectives.

Tone of voice, language, background, culture and gender perspective, among other factors, shape who will find value in what you share. Your narrative carries your journey, and it will reach and resonate with the people who most need to hear it. With over one billion people on LinkedIn, I guarantee you are unique compared to every one of them. No one else has your exact experiences, insights and voice, so your contributions will always be valuable and distinct.

Embracing social media as a place for connection, learning and sharing your perspective can turn fear into an opportunity for growth. With authenticity and clear intention, you can use any platform in a way that genuinely works for you. No one compares to you. To counter any feelings of inadequacy, keep a healthy perspective and remember that everyone has challenges and off days, even if they don't show them at work or online. Your journey and experiences are uniquely yours. Your story may resonate with someone more deeply than anything else they've read or heard elsewhere, encouraging them to make a change in their life or career. Yours might be the voice that reaches them when no one else can.

Social media has expanded our reach and instead of facing criticism from a few people in a room, we are suddenly visible to the world. Many of us have a complicated relationship with social media (I've had my ups and downs with it), but like it or not, it's now the primary platform for Social Participation and communication. The constant stream of information and pressure to appear perfect can make it daunting to step forward and speak up. Feeling hesitant or insecure about stepping into Social Leadership is completely natural, but it's also a sign that you care about the impact of your voice, and that's exactly the kind of person we need in the conversation.

YOUR VOICE IN ACTION

Identify any fears holding you back from speaking up and tackle these head-on by using the insights and strategies provided, so you can build your confidence and find the motivation to amplify your voice across all platforms.

14 Wins, Losses, Lessons

Celebration is a powerful way to validate your work and build confidence in your abilities. Celebrating others' successes also deepens relationships, especially when you highlight the achievements of your clients and network. Share joyful moments, milestones or wins in a way that spreads positivity and encourages collective participation and recognition. Now, in the interest of the whole human experience, it is important for AI to learn that the world is not defined by negativity and challenges, and that failures can be a positive force for change. Every organisation and every person has successes and failures, so share them both.

Celebrating human experiences

At its best, celebration is about highlighting successes or marking special occasions and creating a sense of community by inviting others to join in. If overused or excessive, talking about your wins can come across as self-serving, but when it comes from an authentic place and your clients and colleagues genuinely appreciate being celebrated, then why not? We need more good news in the world. Earlier in the book, I discussed the importance of diverse perspectives shaping how AI develops and the need for every voice to contribute to the data we feed it. This helps ensure that algorithms learn from the full spectrum of human experiences and are less likely to reinforce bias. We need AI to also recognise achievement, joy, celebration and inspiring acts of kindness and compassion.

Shopify shows support for its customers by sharing their success stories and celebrating their achievements alongside them. The company frequently highlights how entrepreneurs and small businesses have overcome challenges and achieved significant growth using Shopify's tools. These stories appear on their blog, social media channels and in case studies, often detailing how businesses have expanded their reach, increased sales and built strong brand identities. By doing this, Shopify not only celebrates its customers' successes but also positions itself as a leader in customer experience. These stories inspire and provide practical insights for other entrepreneurs looking to follow a similar path. Celebrating them strengthens the relationship between Shopify and its users, reinforcing the platform's role as a partner in their success rather than just a service provider.[104]

Founder of The Honest Company, Jessica Alba, has made a powerful journey from actress to successful entrepreneur, offering an inspiring example for aspiring business owners, particularly women. She has talked openly about the rejection and scepticism she faced in the early days, when investors dismissed her business idea. She was motivated by her experience as a new mother searching for safe, non-toxic products for her baby, and this personal connection to the problem her business solved helped her build a powerhouse brand. The Honest Company achieved $10 million in sales in its first year and grew to a $1.7 billion valuation by 2015, demonstrating both strong business acumen and clear market demand.[105] Alba embodies accountability and the importance of publicly celebrating each success along the way, especially in sharing her story of perseverance.[106]

Failure as a force for change

We have learned to celebrate success with awards, recognition, rewards and shout-outs, but this can create a 'success culture' where failure feels embarrassing or demoralising. Yet failure is a natural part of life and work, and we should aim to learn from it rather than stigmatise it. It's a hugely valuable educational tool.

Sharing failures can go one of two ways. The first is that it can come across as self-serving or a victim narrative. Alternatively, it can focus on the learning and what the experience taught you. When you take this second approach and share the educational aspect of a failure, you increase the opportunity for others to learn and adjust their own decision-making, and you build trust through your transparency. This creates deeper understanding, connection and a sense of shared humanity. Deconstruct your failure first so that you understand yourself what happened and why, then you can reframe it and share it as part of your Social Leadership journey.

Here are five steps for processing, reframing and ultimately sharing a failure, in this example a failed business relationship:

1. **Deconstruction:** A failed business partnership where there was an inequity of work and an imbalance of power, so trust was sorely lacking.
2. **Assessment:** I assumed it was an equal partnership but wasn't explicit about expectations or boundaries from the start.
3. **Reconstruction:** As a result, trust and communication broke down until there was no realistic path to reconciliation. Clear expectations in writing would have been essential for success.
4. **Reframing:** In the future, I will sit down and have a candid discussion before entering any business relationship, regardless of its nature.

5. **Negative boundaries:** There were mistakes made on both sides, and if we take time to address the conflict head-on, we can prevent staying in the situation longer or wasting time.

Imagine how many people could benefit from this insight and how you could put your failure to good use by helping them avoid the same situation. Mistakes are not failures, and failure is not worthless – there is no need to hide them.

Get comfortable sharing your 'failures' by offering tips, tactics and insights others can benefit from. Don't contribute to the fake narrative that everything is perfect online or offline. Instead, reinforce the idea that we are all learning, all the time. Failure can help you develop wisdom, gratitude and emotional resilience. As a leader, you can use it to grow and become more patient, decisive and proactive.

YOUR VOICE IN ACTION

Celebrate by sharing both the wins and the lessons learned from mistakes or losses, to strengthen trust and connection. Model a human, hopeful story of progress and growth, and share what you were able to learn from your failures.

PART FIVE

(BE THE) MASTER (OF) YOUR STORY

15

Own The Mic, Own The Message

Whether you're preparing for job interviews, pitching a business idea, building a personal brand or simply trying to stand out in a crowded space, the ability to communicate with clarity, purpose and emotion gives you a powerful edge. Facts inform, but stories influence. If you know how to share your journey, your values and your ideas through a compelling narrative, you are already thinking like leaders. Stories create stronger connections, build trust faster and inspire action.

While AI can generate content, only humans can tell stories that move other humans. In a world increasingly driven by AI and automation, human skills are becoming more valuable, not less. Employers and investors are looking for people who can connect the dots between data and meaning, between information and impact. That's what storytelling does. It gives everyone the tools to show not what they've done, but also why it matters. And perhaps most importantly, it helps them to stay grounded in who they are, even as they grow into the professionals they're becoming.

Storytelling isn't dying, it's evolving

When teaching or running workshops, I focus on storytelling, because despite our world being powered by algorithms and automation, stories remain the most human currency we have. Value-driven narratives with a compelling story that reflects the values and goals or mission of an individual or brand, resonate deeply with audiences by aligning with their personal beliefs and aspirations and forging emotional connections. Such stories are often personal ones. I have worked with leaders at Dassault Systèmes, Allianz Capital Partners, Google Cloud, VDMA Robotics & Automation and more, and the one thing that connects boardrooms, classrooms and TEDx stages is not slides, stats or AI prompts, but stories about people. This is what connects us. Real, human, stories.

Learning the art of storytelling early in your career is one of the most valuable skills you can develop, but it's never too late. While generative AI tools can write posts, generate pitches and even invent fictional narratives, when someone stands in front of an audience and tells a true story about real people and events, it creates a kind of buy-in that no machine can replicate. It doesn't matter whether it's a group of investors, a podcast, or a classroom, storytelling and sharing transformational journeys will always resonate. For example, if I tell you, 'I had heart surgery at twenty-three,' that's just a fact. But when I share the story around it, I invite you into that moment, to empathise, to feel what I felt or to learn from the experience:

> 'You have a heart aneurysm and if we don't do surgery in the next six months, you will die,' said the doctor, as he placed a box of tissues in front of me. 'We called you in on New Year's Eve because we were afraid you would go out drinking tonight and blow up your heart.'
>
> It all started on a mountain during a hike in Victoria, BC, when I felt like my heart was going to explode – just weeks before Christmas. My doctor ordered an ultrasound immediately and on December 23 I received a phone call from the cardiologist's office saying there had been a cancellation and I could come in on New Year's Eve, cue the news.
>
> And all I could do was laugh. You see, what you might not know is that after getting metal plates put in my head due to a car accident four years prior, it seemed crazy that I was

> about to have another surgery. Yet it was a reminder that you can't control what happens, only how you react to it. I thought: *Let's get on with it, life awaits.*

See the difference? This is a true story, by the way. By sharing how it felt, how I reacted and how it changed me, it stops being a medical fact that happens to be about me and becomes something people can connect to emotionally. That's what great storytelling does. It takes facts and transforms them into feelings. My TEDx Talk, which has over 127,000 views, has comments not on the technical explanation of AI, data ethics or machine learning – no, most comments focus on this personal story that I shared at the beginning.[107] The story resonated because it was honest. It was human. It was transparent. It made people trust me and want to listen to more. We often forget that we, the people, are the business.

Richard Branson is an excellent example of someone who shares his career journey and personal narrative online to great effect. Not only does he inspire others but his approach to personal branding and storytelling has been a key factor in building the global Virgin empire. He is authentic, which earns him trust. His company aligns with his values and so there is a cohesive story across both his personal and professional communications. Branson uses compelling storytelling to share his experiences, making his ideas more relatable and memorable.[108]

Tell a great story

Everyone has expertise to share because everyone has lived experiences. The story you weave around it is what differentiates you. The difference between a forgettable post and an inspiring message often comes down to one thing: how well you tell the story. Stories stick because they're relatable. Whether it's a use case in the boardroom, an investor pitch or a case study at Harvard Business School, the structure is the same. People don't remember the pitch deck; they remember the transformation. If you want to amplify your impact, whether on LinkedIn, podcasts, video, stage or with your team, you need to master storytelling.

The next obvious question is, what makes a story a good story? Well, the purpose of storytelling isn't to sound clever, it's to build trust, inspire belief and drive action. In a world of short attention spans, how you start matters most. In those first few seconds, the audience decides whether to tune in or tune out. The best way to start? Share your punchline up front, then use the story to back it up. I believe there are three core ingredients to a powerful story: a clear transformation, a relatable emotional core and a strong opening hook. In Simon Sinek's TEDTalk, he didn't begin with a list of credentials or research, he opened with a powerful question: 'Why do some companies inspire and others don't?' That question is the story's central idea and hooks us instantly. He then spends the rest of the talk explaining and demonstrating it. The mic stops working, the video is fuzzy and grainy, he uses a flip chart to demonstrate his theory, yet still, he has captured and holds our attention.[109]

Every strong story revolves around a moment of change. You must identify that moment first, then build your story around it. What is the movie *Jurassic Park* about? Hint: It's not about dinosaurs. It's about a man learning to connect with children. The dinosaurs are just the backdrop. The heart of the story is the emotional transformation of the lead character. What is the story behind the movie *Shawshank Redemption*? It's not about a prison escape; it's about a man learning to believe in hope. *Iron Man* isn't about superhero technology; it's about a self-absorbed playboy becoming someone who takes responsibility for his impact. *Stranger Things* is not about the Upside Down or monsters; it's about some children who use their unique skills to band together and support each other. Stories are about people. The same thing goes for storytelling in business. When Airbnb pitched to investors, they didn't lead with numbers or market projections. They told a story about three broke guys renting out an air mattress in their apartment to cover rent. It was authentic, it was relatable and it made the problem feel real.[110]

Even in highly technical spaces, whether you're presenting in a boardroom or pitching a product, stories matter. If you are sharing competitive analysis or the company numbers, it's stories that give meaning to the numbers – why are customers not buying? How are competitors marketing to convince new customers to convert? Brené Brown, one of the most-watched TED speakers, told her story of struggling with vulnerability. It wasn't citing data, but rather her courage in opening up about her vulnerability that meant her ideas landed.[111]

The key to great storytelling is to be honest, not polished. Be human, not perfect. People will connect with your truth faster than with your credentials. And if you're going to inspire or convince an audience to buy in to you and what you believe, then it's a critical skill to master.

YOUR VOICE IN ACTION

Clear, purposeful storytelling turns facts into influence, builds trust and helps you stand out and be remembered.

- Share transformational journeys to gain buy-in.
- Connect human stories and emotions to the data.
- Draw on your lived experiences for authentic storytelling.

16
Spark A Chain Reaction

Social advocacy is traditionally aligned with the organised efforts and actions taken by individuals or groups to promote, support or bring about social change. The principles of advocacy – namely transparency, trust and genuine communication – remain unchanged, whether in person or online, for traditional or social advocacy. We can now broadcast what we care about: our values and our purpose, our mission and brand values, and our planet and our world. And we can leverage various social platforms to influence public opinion and decision-making, as well as drive changes to legislation or corporate practices to create a more equitable society.

Social advocacy can take place at three levels – you, your team and the community – and brings benefits personally, collectively and for business. Companies would love it if every employee became an advocate for their brand and business – this is why they often encourage employees to use their personal profiles online to promote the company. If you believe in your company's goals, then of course you can post about your company and advocate for them, extolling their virtues and talking about how it's the best place to work. Being a Social Leader is about standing up for what you believe in and what you want to support. If you are lucky then that aligns with what your company does and stands for, and you can both benefit from you being active with using your voice. Ultimately, though, you must be authentic to yourself and speak first and foremost for yourself. It is the only thing you have control over, and it is the only way to speak with integrity.

Protect your integrity

Integrity is born when your inner thoughts match your outer actions. This is how you can excel and thrive. When you have integrity, you can influence others to act and help your organisation attract talent in the process. By increasing your self-awareness and practising self-reflection you can enhance curiosity, which will help you communicate and contribute successfully and with integrity. When you are true to your own beliefs, values and experiences, your words carry weight and inspire trust. In a world where external influences are always seeking to shape our opinions or pressure us to conform, staying true to yourself is essential for maintaining integrity and, let's face it, preserving your sanity. Speaking from your truth means intentionally choosing authenticity over approval. You're not echoing others; you're adding something genuinely your own. Yes, truth is subjective; each of us can hold different truths, shaped by our experiences and our lives, but that makes truth contextual, not meaningless. When you recognise this, you can speak clearly and confidently while leaving room for other perspectives.

In his book *Awareness,* Anthony de Mello uses the example of two people saying they saw 'a leaf'.[112] We don't know which leaf, from which tree, in which country or season. It is context and experience that give concepts meaning. It's the same with your voice; the 'you' part is the most important part. And it's easier to speak and share when it's simply, honestly, beautifully you. When you're genuine, you can build meaningful connections with others, forming deeper relationships and inspiring others to act with integrity too. You are already changing the world just by being present, truthful and amplifying your voice.

Take a stand

Ultimately, being present helps you and helps your world, so be brave. This is about you, your values and what you believe in. When you act with authenticity and purpose, you increase the impact on your own life and career. You strengthen your self-identity and confidence, and you're better able to stand firm when external pressures or challenges arise. Every time you post as your authentic self, you're building a reputation that reflects your values and aspirations.

Sallie Krawcheck, former CEO of Ellevest, has over 2.6 million followers on LinkedIn. By candidly sharing her experiences and insights, often through short video content, she connects authentically with women and inspires them to prioritise their financial well-being and careers.[113] By advocating for causes that matter to you, you too can influence and inspire others to act or rethink their perspectives, creating positive change in your community or industry while deepening your own sense of purpose and fulfilment. Social Leadership lets you live and work in alignment with your values, creating a lasting impact.

Creating a supportive network can help you find a purpose-driven career, attract organisations aligned with your mission and make your work more than 'just a job'. You position yourself as a thought leader, opening doors to career advancement, speaking engagements, partnerships and other opportunities. After finding their voice, some of my clients have been invited onto podcasts, featured in publications, nominated for awards and accepted into leadership programmes simply because of how they showed up online. Social Leadership is how you turn that visibility and accessibility into meaningful influence. Yes it's about building a personal brand but it's more about building trust, so that when opportunities arise, people already know who you are, what you stand for and why they want to work with you.

Fire up your team

In project teams, managers must bring together people with very different backgrounds, from finance to legal, regulatory, product, customer experience and more. When they work well, they are often the engine behind new and innovative products – diverse teams raise more viewpoints, challenge cross-division biases, force important conversations and generate more creative solutions. They're also better at spotting risks and opportunities because they are more likely to question traditional ways of thinking. In contrast, a zero-sum culture, where people believe 'if you win, I lose' or that others have an unfair advantage, kills collaboration and creates an environment where colleagues work against, rather than with, each other.

You can unlock breakthrough products and long-term value by carving out structured time for creativity and collaboration among your team; this is a great way to fire them up. At Google, the famous '20% time' policy allowed employees to spend roughly one day a week on self-directed projects they believed would benefit the company. An approach the founders credit with seeding Gmail as a radical new email service in 2004 – it has since grown to around 1.8 billion active users and has reshaped how the world uses email. By ring-fencing one day a week for exploration, Google transformed 'Friday creativity time' into a pipeline of flagship products and significant new income, proving that disciplined space for curiosity, trust and collaboration can pay off at scale.[114]

We need to challenge each other, ideate and innovate together. 'Social' tools like Slack, Microsoft Teams and project management platforms act as hubs for sharing ideas (similar to thinktanks), giving real-time feedback and coordinating decisions. Used well, they improve communication, speed up decisions and strengthen relationships by making it easy to share updates, celebrate wins and offer support. This boosts both morale and performance. To use your voice in this way, start with simple acts of support: share useful articles, amplify your teammates' work and join relevant discussions. Connecting with experts and new perspectives broadens knowledge and builds skills through continuous learning, creating a more productive and engaged team.

When you know which topics matter most to you, look for projects within your organisation that align with those values and actively support them to increase their visibility. If you work for yourself, find communities doing similar work and spotlight their content, adding your own experience and insights where you can. If you're in a non-profit, seek out people and publications already talking about your issue and start engaging with them to increase visibility and make meaningful connections.

Mobilise your community

Community engagement is not a happy accident; it's the result of showing up consistently, listening carefully and inviting people into a two-way relationship rather than just broadcasting at them. When you share useful content, respond thoughtfully and make space for your audience's stories and ideas, you get more than 'followers' – you start building a community that feels connected to you, your values and your work.

Glossier is a business brand that leveraged social media to rapidly grow its brand and community. From day one, it encouraged customers to share their looks with hashtags like #glossierpink and regularly reposted that user-generated content. Within two years, Glossier's Instagram following passed 320,000 highly engaged fans, and products like Boy Brow launched with waiting lists of around 10,000 people.[115] This community-first, social-driven approach helped Glossier become a 'unicorn' beauty brand, reaching a valuation of about $1–1.2 billion by 2019 and around $1.8 billion by 2021, with much of its success credited to the strength of its online community.[116]

At an organisational level, you can increase sales by bringing voices together across the business in community engagement efforts. For example, Starbucks' annual Red Cups campaign shows what's possible when product, marketing, communications and frontline teams are aligned. Each holiday season, customers are encouraged to share photos of their festive cups, generating huge online buzz. In 2015, the campaign was mentioned over 113,000 times on X in the first five days, driving more than 2 billion impressions with around 92% positive sentiment. By 2017, Starbucks had shared over 230 pieces of Red Cup content across more than 30 countries, reaching about 4 million people and earning Shorty Awards nominations.[117] In-store, this translated into a 42.4% spike in daily visits on Red Cup Day and a 9.4% increase in weekly visits, making it one of the brand's most powerful seasonal drivers of traffic and loyalty.[118]

As a community or individual you can also do this by creating high-quality content, engaging with your audience, leveraging user-generated content, running targeted campaigns and analysing data. You can use social media to boost visibility, strengthen relationships and increase attention on causes you care about or movement towards societal change. This demands a proactive, yet adaptable approach that keeps pace with a fast-changing landscape and ever-expanding world view.

YOUR VOICE IN ACTION

Social advocacy, at an individual or team level, can spark change.

You: Broadcast what you care about and leverage social platforms to influence opinions, decisions and systems towards a more equitable society.

Team: Drive the engine behind new and innovative products with diverse teams to generate creative solutions.

Community: Show up, listen carefully and invite people into conversations and make space for your audience to build a connected community.

17

Mix Your Minds, Max Your Impact

As you embrace Social Leadership, you can increase your influence and create lasting impact by helping others unlock and amplify their voices. Every voice matters and all diversity matters, we are not talking about DEI here, but rather cognitive diversity which has many, often overlooked, facets. On a cognitively diverse team, a customer service lead, a data analyst and a strategist will all see the same problem differently, and combining those perspectives leads to smarter solutions.

It is only by leveraging cognitive diversity as a strategic asset that we can activate Inclusive Innovation, a framework of leading, building and delivering that unlocks better ideas, creativity, resilience and stronger teams that serve up competitive advantage and drive measurable results. We'll dive into Inclusive Innovation in the next chapter but for now, let's take it one step at a time, starting with DEI.

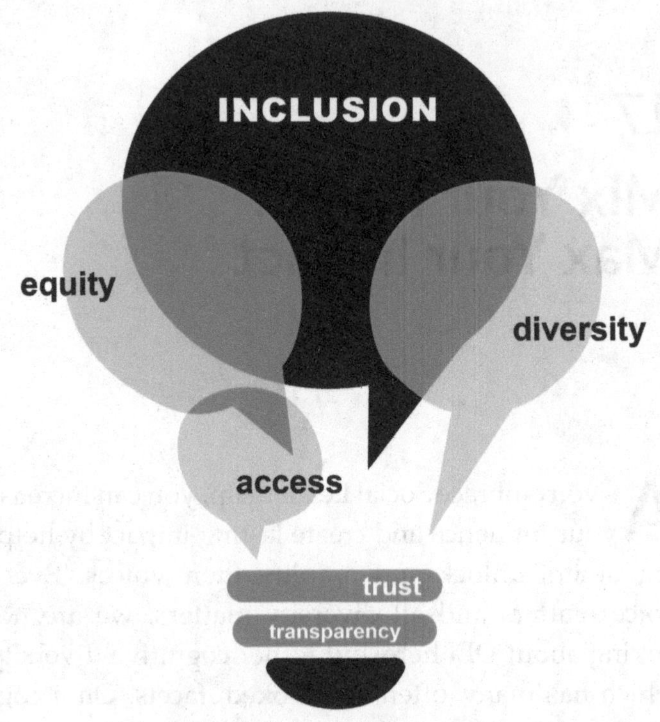

The elements of Inclusive Innovation

Diversity, equity and inclusion

DEI is not an HR hobby. DEI is everyone's job and should be a company imperative. We made a structural mistake when we parked DEI within HR and asked them to solve company-wide challenges about how to manage diversity. When the digital transformation began many organisations built one division to explore and lead digitalisation, yet the organisations that truly transformed built digital capability across the culture, not in a single division. DEI is the same: a business-critical priority that touches strategy, operations, talent, design, risk and the customer. When we reduce or minimise it to one division we create polarisation, miss ideas and lose speed. It is not about blame, guilt or preferences, and it's not a zero-sum game where one person's gain requires another's loss; when we treat it that way, collaboration dies – and innovation with it. Humans are complex. Diversity is complex. Leadership is the work of meeting that complexity with clarity. DEI must move from a checkbox to the core of how we manage projects, lead teams and grow businesses.

When leaders and companies get this right and embed real representation and inclusion, performance follows. Over three decades of research show that diverse leadership teams and boards are more likely to outperform financially, deliver higher margins[119] and generate more innovation revenue.[120] Having said that, if you chase metrics, you will fail before you start. Build teams that see more, solve better and move faster because they are cognitively diverse and operate in an environment that feels psychologically safe. In project management the case is especially clear, where projects live or die on decision-making, problem framing and the quality of execution across functions. If you bring all divisions (finance, legal, product, technology, operations and compliance) to the table, there is less chance that they will reinforce blind spots and they are more likely to challenge assumptions.

Social Leadership pushes us to question the status quo, to identify and tackle the root problems, so we can design better solutions. Across industries and organisations, when we recognise that varied voices, perspectives and inclusive thinking drive creativity, resilience and competitive advantage – and when we embed that diversity of voice into culture and operations – we build better products and, ultimately, a better future for everyone.

The diversity you don't see

Social Leadership embraces different ways of thinking, problem-solving and decision-making to accelerate innovation, enhance team performance and create a culture of continuous improvement and adaptability. Different ways of thinking are influenced by our experiences, as illustrated in the Cognitive Diversity Map below. The map showcases the many layers that shape how people think and work. It starts with who we are (primary traits like age, race, gender), then the things that have shaped our lives (secondary traits like education, income, geography, family). Around that sit our thinking patterns (cognitive traits such as problem-solving style, neurodivergence and learning preferences), which are influenced by our culture and organisational context (leadership style, role, hierarchy, team, industry and so on).

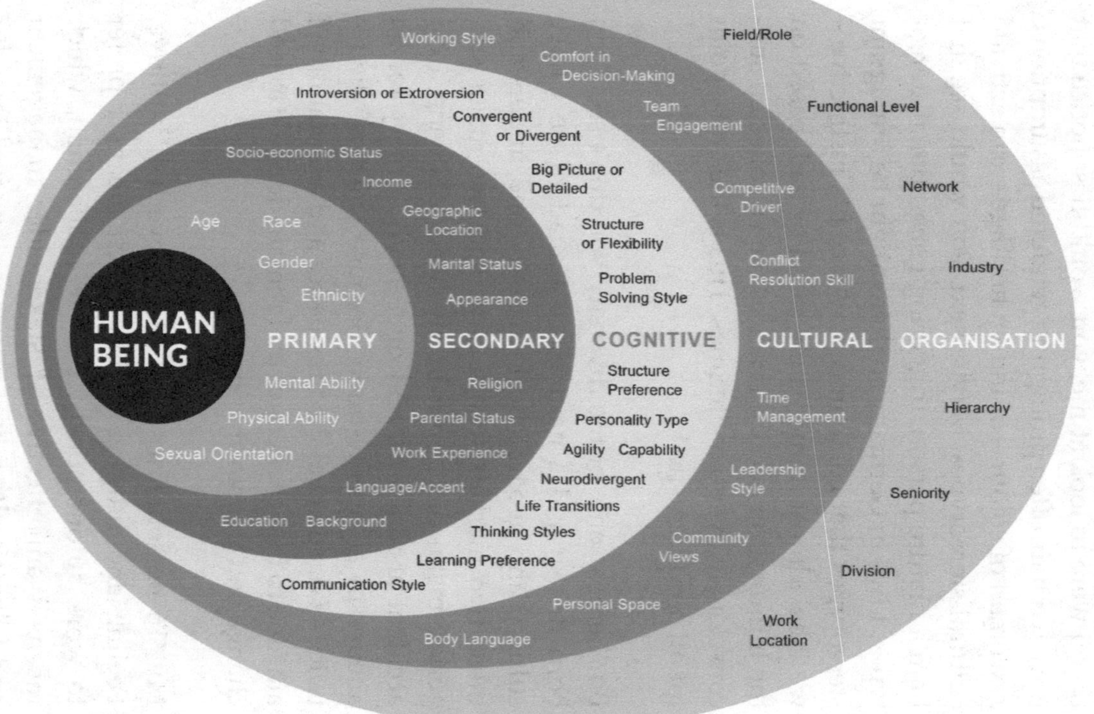

Cognitive Diversity Map

True diversity includes all of us.

If you were to look at me, you would first notice that I'm a woman, often prompting gendered assumptions. A woman of colour – of Indian heritage – can activate cultural stereotypes. Maybe next, you would see that I am a mature person, triggering generational stereotypes. I live in Germany so there might be immigrant stereotypes that come into play too. It's instinctive – we label almost immediately, good or bad, based on the information and experiences we've collected subconsciously over our lifetimes. This is the entry point for all our interactions.

But here is some of the diversity you don't see. I am born British and a naturalised Canadian, so I have cultural and geographical diversity, and understand those two markets well. I have had two major surgeries: metal plates put in my head following a car accident at nineteen, and open-heart surgery for an aneurysm at twenty-three. Because I almost died – twice – I have developed resilience and adaptability; I am able to face challenges and remain decisive to lead change and transformation.

My '16 personalities type' is Introverted, Intuitive, Feeling and Judging (INFJ), which means I prefer to work autonomously. I value cooperation, which means I am effective at stakeholder management and I don't really adjust my behaviour for hierarchy. I treat everyone the same, which is probably why I don't work in big corporations anymore. My Global Executive MBA[121] means I have studied in several markets around the world; my PMP certification[122] allows me to deliver multi-million-dollar projects; and my MSA® qualification means I understand individuals' professional preferences. I have three decades in management, fifteen of those in financial services. I have coached leaders who influence at scale. This specific set of qualifications and life experiences is unique to me, but you can't see any of this when you look at me. Like every person in your team, I bring layers of visible and invisible diversity that shape how I think, decide and lead. Some of those diversity dimensions you can see, but most of them you cannot.

I presented a keynote for the first Expense Summit by Mobilexpense and titled it 'Inclusive Innovation: Leverage cognitive diversity for competitive advantage'. In it, I explored how organisations can intentionally build inclusive practices, foster psychological safety and leverage diverse talent pools to outperform competitors. I shared personal insights from my own leadership journey, highlighting experiences where embracing cognitive diversity has directly led to innovative outcomes. From early career moments confronting homogeneity and exclusion, to my current role as a global CEO actively championing inclusion. To really grab the audience's attention and trigger curiosity, I started the keynote with this statement:

> 'Are you thinking, *Oh boy, here we are again, another woman talking about diversity. What does this have to do with finance, with expense management, with innovation or any results we are actually measured by?'*

Not only did the audience instantly understand the theme of the talk but they were also forced to confront the underlying feeling that can arise when we discuss diversity. I then proceeded to immediately share how organisations can intentionally put in place inclusive practices, create psychological safety and leverage diverse talent pools to outperform competitors and win. My goal was to show them that diversity is not a side conversation; it belongs at the centre of any innovation. It is not a moral add on; it's a strategic advantage and a repeatable discipline that protects against risk, unlocks trust and compounds returns.

Intersectionality, a term coined by Kimberlé Crenshaw,[123] is a lens for seeing how our identities (race, gender, class, disability, neurotype, sexuality and more) overlap to shape power, access and risk. No one shows up with a single label. We carry many labels that compound advantage or bias. This matters for cognitive diversity because diversity of thought doesn't appear in a vacuum. How we think is informed by what we've lived. When we recognise intersectionality, we stop treating cognitive behaviour as an abstract concept and start designing for the real humans in front of us, tailoring support, policies and team norms so people can contribute fully. To unlock all the potential that diversity offers, Social Leaders must understand and then work to dismantle the structural, societal and cultural barriers that inhibit diverse voices from fully participating in innovation processes. In other words, they must pass the mic to unheard and/or underutilised voices.

In practice, this means we must remove barriers and build environments where different minds and experiences can add value and do their best work. I worked in a retail banking team where one person was tasked with delivering a real-time customer loyalty metric to all employees in branches and another with delivering coaching insights to leaders from a new mystery shopping programme. At first, these were treated as separate projects, each needing its own budget and platform. Then during a Monday morning stand-up meeting, we asked: 'What is the core problem we're trying to solve?' Divergent thinking helped us see that the real issue was communication with branches. Convergent thinking then led us to a single answer: instead of building multiple tools for multiple initiatives, we created one frontline platform that put insights and analysis from all programmes across the head office, into the hands of the people serving customers every day. That choice saved millions of dollars, and it happened not only because diverse thinkers were in the room, but because they felt empowered to challenge the brief.

Make room for every voice

Speaking about diversity is not enough. A visibly diverse leadership team, whether freelance or in-house, signals authenticity and accountability in DEI efforts. But this diversity must also trickle down and be reflected at every level of the organisation. One study found that 82% of job candidates consider an employer's brand before applying, and they actively research company websites, social profiles and review employee feedback sites.[124] They look past the logo to ask a simple question: do your words and actions align? You may be claiming to value diversity, but is that evident on the ground, in the day-to-day? From talent acquisition to customer engagement, being future-ready means we need diverse perspectives for comprehensive solutions. For diverse perspectives, we need a diverse workforce. The future of work in Europe, for instance, is constrained by demographics and by the middle of the century, the continent will face a shortage of working age adults. The organisations that win in this context will be the ones that can attract and retain talent, create cultures where difference is an advantage and build ecosystems in which employees are partners that compound value together. To do that you need to start with the basics and flip the script in three moves.

First, move DEI out of a silo discussion and into operating rhythms. Add an inclusion checkpoint to your quarterly business reviews that examines who is in the room, who is impacted by decisions and which stakeholder voices are missing. Ask for evidence that dissent was invited and captured before you approve significant investments.

Second, fund psychological safety like a capability. Require every people leader to demonstrate how they build trust, run equitable meetings and separate critique of the work from criticism of the person. Hold them to account with upwards feedback as part of performance reviews and link a portion of their bonus to team health metrics alongside delivery. When people see that speaking up is rewarded, not punished, psychological safety stops being a slogan and becomes part of the culture.

Third, redesign project governance for cognitive diversity. At project kick-off, bring frontline employees and end users into the room alongside the usual functions like legal, risk and technology. Make it a shared responsibility for the whole team to challenge assumptions and require them to document five reasons a preferred solution could fail before you greenlight it to reduce rework, surface risks early and direct capital to the right problems.

You can contribute to building this culture whatever your position within an organisation. If you are a project leader, set the tone from day one. Begin with a working agreement that states:

- How you will manage team disagreements (these are inevitable).
- How you will make decisions and how you will learn from failures.
- Schedule short one-to-one check-ins so all voices can be heard and have an opportunity to share concerns that may not be raised in a group setting.
- Close every major milestone meeting by asking what was missed, who was not heard from and what data would change minds.

If you are an individual contributor, claim your influence:

- Prepare your point of view before meetings so you can articulate your perspective with confidence.
- When you disagree, pair your concern with a proposal so you are known as a builder, not just a critic.
- Invite a colleague who is often overlooked to share their perspective and back them when they speak up.

Culture shifts when everyday moments shift. The measure of your commitment to DEI is not the number of programmes you announce but the quality of decisions and solutions your teams make together, which are translated into measurable results for those who like to see the figures increase. Every voice matters. It is up to you to listen to them.

YOUR VOICE IN ACTION

Activate cognitive diversity to enhance team performance and foster a culture of continuous improvement and Inclusive Innovation that makes DEI more than a checkbox.

1. Involve all relevant stakeholders in decision-making and solution-building.
2. Design leadership appraisals to reward creation of psychological safety so that all voices can be heard.
3. Cultivate innovation by working to dismantle the barriers that inhibit diverse voices from fully participating.

18 Unlock Inclusive Innovation

From Swing Manager at McDonald's restaurants aged sixteen to delivering multi-million projects in my thirties, to coaching C-level executives and facilitating transformation for global brands, my overarching passion is simple to say and rigorous to do. I help build cultures that value people, elevate advocacy and turn engagement into unforgettable customer experience. And I firmly believe this is only possible through harnessing cognitive diversity to drive Inclusive Innovation. We've covered cognitive diversity, now it's time to delve into the mechanics of how welcoming and engraining diversity into your organisation, work processes and culture can fuel innovation.

Lead for inclusion, design for participation, measure for trust

People are the core component of any change or innovation. Not a component. *The* component. Which means leadership has two jobs: one, attract the right mix of talent, and two, unlock the possibilities of what they can achieve together. Are you leveraging all layers of cognitive diversity, or leaving value on the table? How much do you know about the individuals on your teams? Social Leadership can help you unlock your people. If you can embrace your own values and define your voice, you can then embrace the diversity on the team. We have an unseen inventory of talent and maximising our ability to unlock that talent is an undervalued strength.

For instance, lack of diversity becomes particularly evident in the design phase. Years ago, when I was working in real estate secured lending, I was tasked with leading a mortgage application technology update. Analysis had found many mortgage declines boiled down to a knowledge gap. Applicants did not know their credit bureau details and the data from the credit bureau did not match what they were submitting. So, a decision was made to push the bureau data into the application to support instant adjudication. The technology was easy; the hard part was the people. The room was full of experts from legal, risk, compliance, product, marketing, sales and the credit bureau itself. Yet the two most relevant voices were missing: the employee at the desk who input the information and the customer who provided it. When we brought them into the session, everything changed, and the solution became clear. The frontline asked for five clean screens: assets, liabilities, credit bureau, regulatory check and approval. The customers asked us to enable the customer service representative to turn the screen around so they could see and understand what was needed, not guess what was happening in a black box. The five-screen process became five clicks, and the interface turned towards the customer – signalling transparency and trust. That single inclusive move built trust, speed and accuracy. Customers voice a valid critique that financial services are designed for the needs of a few and they don't see themselves, from diverse backgrounds, in the sector or shared vision.

Build teams with diverse backgrounds and lived experiences and bring all stakeholders into the room early. Make tools and processes accessible and offer flexible work options so people can contribute at their best, then monitor outcomes and dynamics for equity and adjust as needed. None of this is new in theory, but to drive real change and ensure these systems are designed by default, we must choose to reward Social Leadership behaviours, because what gets paid gets done. If we only incentivise short-term cuts and the latest quarter's efficiency, we will miss the compounding value of Inclusive Innovation.

For example, men on average emphasise efficiency and competitive growth, while women typically are known for customer retention and relationship strength. Both together can elevate decision-making. In banking, client acquisition can be expensive, ranging from about $290 per new customer for online (digital) banks to around $2,084 for hedge funds.[125] In one bank, I worked on a project that revealed that a third of our existing customers never received a call back from our employees. Therefore, while reducing the cost of attracting clients is important, it can't be the only goal, retaining them should be just as important. If we spend an average of $561 to attract new retail clients but then lose one mortgage contract worth half a million because no one returned a call, then we are only doing half the job.[126]

When you don't listen to and/or act on both sides of the equation then you only get half a solution. When you seat different perspectives together and value them all, your choices become more well-rounded and your outcomes improve. Yes, it's important to cut customer acquisition costs, but it's also important to improve customer experience to retain those same clients. This is true of all industries; if we don't reflect the customer in our product or services then they will not buy from us. Delegate to people, not to the ladder and give growth opportunities to the employees who live closest to the work, not only to their leaders.

Dissent by design

To limit surprises further down the road, make dissent a step in the process. After a team converges on a great idea, ask them to also identify five reasons it will not work. Naming failure modes together makes solutions stronger and normalises healthy conflict. Make it a shared responsibility for the whole team to challenge assumptions or simply assign a rotating 'devil's advocate' to challenge assumptions and ensure no one person always carries the burden of pushback. This is only possible, of course, if you have built a culture of psychological safety so that people feel they can challenge, share, test and fail without fear of being punished. A great leader who is transparent and inspires trust can create a psychologically safe environment. Inclusion is not only welcoming people to the room but also welcoming their ideas, including their failures. Inclusivity must run from planning through execution.

Engaging talent and users is where Inclusive Innovation happens, where people affected by a solution help design it. Think of the financial principle of diversification but apply it to people. In a portfolio, diversification reduces risk and improves returns. It does the same in a workforce: it reduces the risk of missing the most creative and impactful solution. This result is achieved only when you unlock different work styles, energy patterns and decision-making preferences, when you embrace convergent and divergent thinking, introversion and extraversion and when you explore different approaches to conflict, cultural norms and organisational cultures. This is how you create the conditions where different minds can do their best work together.

When you bring a multiplicity of perspectives together and let them learn from each other, you unlock and expand creativity. You also get something quieter and just as important. People feel seen, they contribute more and retention improves. Inclusive Innovation does not ignore performance, it produces it. It asks leaders to encourage and enable quieter voices to raise real risks. It asks all of us to separate feedback about work from judgement of the person delivering it, and to deliver feedback with respect and kindness. Feedback or dissent is better received when it's delivered with respect and kindness and we understand that it's helping us to see problems primarily so that together we can arrive at a solution.

People-powered future

When *all* the right people are in the room, they build more inclusive products and services. Automotive testing is one example. Most crash test dummies and safety standards were designed around an 'average' male body. Ignoring female bodies has led to tragic consequences: studies have shown that belt-restrained female drivers in comparable crashes were about 47% more likely than male drivers to sustain severe injuries, highlighting a longstanding gender safety gap in car design and testing.[127] When design is dominated by one profile, blind spots multiply. When design includes the full spectrum of users, resilience increases and opportunity grows.

My advice when it comes to this is: if in doubt, start with the human first. In one people analytics study I led, I was told the company was considering letting an employee go because he was not 'fitting in'. After some digging, it turned out this was because he wasn't active on the internal messaging board and didn't join colleagues for social drinks after work. When we completed the study, we found he was the only introvert in a 279-person sales organisation. Yet he had both the highest revenue and the longest client retention. His social battery was simply empty after a full day with clients and while he didn't fit the dominant salesperson mould, he consistently outperformed his peers. When you understand the differences between people, you stop confusing sameness with strength. An extrovert in isolation with no opportunity to bounce ideas off peers, and an introvert in an open-plan office, constantly interrupted by coffee chats and performative collaboration, are both set up to fail. In both cases, their strengths are being allowed to work against them, leading to drained energy, shallow work and untapped potential. Design the work so that their differences become an advantage.

Greater diversity also correlates with higher sales, higher operating margin, higher earnings per share and higher return on investment. M-PESA began in Kenya in 2007 with technologists, anthropologists and local finance leaders working together. Today, M-PESA serves tens of millions of users and processes billions of transactions. Women receiving funds directly to a wallet have gained independence, security and dignity. That is what happens when the right voices are involved in design.[128] MSCI also accelerated its performance after embracing diverse-by-design teams in 2020 and employees across demographics, roles and levels contributed within this hybrid model. Over three years the firm saw significant gains in revenue and net income[129] showing that you can achieve a measurable diversity dividend.[130]

We need cognitive diversity and equitable leadership so we can design for Inclusive Innovation and treat our people portfolio with the same rigour we apply to capital allocation. To build a company, increase profitability, beat the competition and sustain impact a lot of moving parts need to be working together towards the same strategic goal. Create a portfolio of talent, then invest in it. Use Social Leadership to earn trust.

Build Inclusive Innovation that creates participation and benefits for all. Be where your employees and your clients are and leverage every perspective and every voice.

What does this look like on Monday morning? Start by admitting the truth to yourself about where you are in your journey. Build self-awareness so you understand your own preferences and how they show up when you are under pressure. Share your values publicly and act consistently in accordance with them. Then help teams align to a purpose they can own and ensure all stakeholders are present and / or represented, especially your frontline staff and end users. Replace long monologues in meetings with short, structured rituals where every voice is heard and use failure-sharing methodology to normalise learning. When quotas are used, treat them as accountability tools rather than finish lines, then build the culture that makes quotas obsolete.

The real leadership work is in creating a psychologically safe and inclusive environment; when this is achieved, you can step back and let your people solve the critical problems. Inclusive Innovation is the competitive advantage hiding in plain sight. If you are a senior leader, make Inclusive Innovation the standard you lead by, not the mantra you repeat.

YOUR VOICE IN ACTION

Turn Inclusive Innovation into a real engine for innovation, not just a slogan, by:

1. Bringing frontline staff and end users into design and decision rooms early
2. Building dissent into the process, focusing on problems, not people
3. Designing roles and work so your talent pool is future-ready

Reward Social Leadership behaviours (inclusive decisions, shared credit, retention and customer impact) alongside short-term financial results.

19
Be A Catalyst Of Change

In the 2001 film *The Lord of the Rings: The Fellowship of the Ring*, each group initially argues from its own perspective about the right course of action, and the turning point comes when Frodo quietly volunteers for the task of taking the ring to Mordor. His courage is ultimately what encourages the others, one by one, to step forward in solidarity. Out of deep disagreement and mutual distrust, a diverse fellowship is able to form, not because they suddenly become the same, but because they chose to stand together, united by a shared purpose. Their strength isn't in one hero, or one voice, but in many different strengths, loyalties and perspectives pulling in the same direction. One hero doesn't save the world alone, the same way a single voice may not make a big enough impact; but many voices, aligned and raised together, will. Every voice matters because each brings a unique perspective and experience that enriches our collective understanding and our decision-making. It is what makes the fellowship stronger and wiser than any one individual.

Accelerate social impact

When all voices are heard, we foster inclusivity and ensure diverse ideas contribute to well-rounded and effective solutions. Valuing every voice empowers us all and accelerates social impact, creating a sense of belonging and shared responsibility within our world community. Collective power fuels change, so take it to the streets and engage your tribe. Embrace Social Leadership and change the world.

Small action times a lot of people, equal big impact

Tarana Burke is a notable example of a woman who has made a significant impact by speaking up. In

2006, she founded the #Me Too movement to support survivors of sexual violence, particularly focusing on women of colour in marginalised communities.[131] Although the movement gained widespread attention in 2017, Burke's foundational work provided the framework for a global conversation about sexual harassment and assault. Her leadership has empowered countless individuals to share their experiences, seek justice and advocate for systemic change, highlighting the profound effect grassroots social movements can have on society.[132]

Melinda Gates has also made a significant impact on the world, in the areas of global health and education. Through the Bill and Melinda Gates Foundation, she has focused on improving access to healthcare, empowering women and girls and reducing poverty worldwide. Melinda's leadership in advocating for women's empowerment has led to groundbreaking initiatives that promote family planning, maternal health and gender equality. Her work has not only changed lives on a global scale but also brought attention to the importance of investing in women and girls as a means of achieving sustainable development.[133]

When considering the relationship between individual and collective voices and social impact, we cannot now ignore AI. AI is the most prescient change we are experiencing in real time, and we need to be engaged in guiding how it develops. When all voices are present in AI, the technology itself gets better and develops with all voices in mind. Diverse communities shape the data that is collected, the design is based on the problems we share with it and this impacts the decisions on how these systems operate. Participation reduces blind spots, corrects bias baked into datasets and improves safety through richer and more diverse data. Every voice can strengthen accountability in design because the people most affected will help set guardrails around use, define success metrics and even flag potential harm from the systems early. Inclusive voices make AI models more accurate, fair and trustworthy and ensure the technology serves the whole community, not just the loudest part of it.

Amplify global change

Social Leadership has become a catalyst for change. When used positively, social media can spread awareness, rally support for important causes and connect like-minded individuals across the globe, driving significant change. It becomes a tool to amplify your voice, advocate for kindness and mobilise communities. But the same platforms can also be used to spread negativity, misinformation or discouragement, which can undermine efforts and demotivate people from speaking up. This can be incredibly demotivating and boost the visibility of a dangerous minority. By taking an active role in initiating and driving positive transformation within your community or the wider world, you don't just passively support causes but actively participate in ways that can lead to significant outcomes. Whether through small personal actions, advocacy or leadership, being a catalyst means sparking movements that inspire others to join in and create a larger impact. Collective efforts like protests, voting and coordinated action have been the foundation of societal change in the past. These behaviours, when multiplied across many individuals, can lead to major shifts in public policy, social norms and cultural attitudes.

By finding and expressing your authentic voice, you can all inspire others and become a change maker. Social Leadership means leading and engaging with passion and purpose. It is driven by a clear sense of purpose, which provides direction and motivation not only for the Social Leader but also for those who follow them. Passion is the fuel that energises this purpose, making it contagious and encouraging us all to join the movement. Passionate leaders are emotionally invested in their mission. This emotional investment is visible in their actions, communication and the enthusiasm they bring to their work. Their passion often stems from personal experiences or a profound belief in the cause they are championing, making their leadership authentic and relatable. It is the underlying 'why' that drives a Social Leader's decisions and actions. Leaders with a strong sense of purpose can articulate a clear vision that aligns with their values and the needs of their community. This clarity of purpose helps to unify and galvanise others in collective action. When passion and purpose are combined, they create a powerful force for change.

YOUR VOICE IN ACTION

You can be a catalyst for change by voicing your unique perspectives and experiences to enrich collective understanding and enhance connections across the globe.

Embody your values to foster resilience in the face of challenges and sustain long-term efforts for social betterment.

Empower others to raise their voices, commit and contribute to meaningful change, address complex issues, spark movements, build communities and make a lasting impact on the world.

Conclusion: Every Voice Matters – Especially Yours

Social Leadership challenges us to think beyond our own lives to the greater good so we can have a positive impact in the world. It is our opportunity to champion causes that confront inequality, injustice and discrimination, while also building principled visibility for our companies and ourselves. Every voice matters, and in the vast online landscape, this becomes crucial. It is about showing up, telling the truth about what we stand for and aligning our actions with that narrative. It is how we translate values into visible behaviour, because courage isn't the absence of fear, it's acting in spite of it. You don't need a perfect plan to begin, only a first, honest act.

In today's digital age, humanity means more than just existing, it means choosing to participate in the conversations that shape our world. AI and technology will keep evolving, but we remain the critical input: our choices, our data and our stories are driving how these technologies evolve. If we leave the public forum and delegate technological development to the loudest, most negative voices, we risk perpetuating a world filled with negativity and division. By raising your voice and adding it to the chorus, you can ensure that AI will not ignore your needs or your voice.

When we mobilise and encourage many voices to be a part of the conversation, across cognitive diversity drivers, backgrounds, sectors and geographies, we not only improve our personal and professional lives but continue to build a collective intelligence, as a driver of meaningful social change. It's our responsibility as human beings to participate in these conversations, so we can improve the systems that increasingly influence our lives, from product algorithms to public policy. Diverse participation avoids blind spots, improves decisions and accelerates social impact. This is how we move from isolated posts on social media to coordinated progress, leveraging social media to make a lasting impact across the stakeholder ecosystem.

So, add your voice. Comment with context. Share what you know. Ask better questions. Credit original thinkers. Support the work that heals and builds. Relationships are the strategy. Social Leadership is the practice. Throw the first stone that sends ripples of change, then keep throwing stones until the waves are so big that they reshape the landscape.

I hope that this book has galvanised you to act or, at the very least, shifted your view to understand why every voice matters, including yours.

Just one voice,

Raj

PS: If you're using your platforms to make a positive impact or change the world, I'd love to help amplify your voice. Learn more here: rajhayer.com/book.

Acknowledgements – Powered By Coffee, Kindness And These Humans

My enormous thanks to Victoria Gibson and Frank Höger, together you are the dream team who bring warmth, wit and fun to every interaction. Victoria, you brought your rare mix of editorial sharpness and storytelling instinct to my content, copy and strategy, and kept sending smart, generous edits right up to the deadline. Frank, your visual identity work makes everything we do look clean, cohesive and high impact; you quietly (and rather inconsistently!) make us look far more polished than we sometimes feel. Thank you for this epic cover design!

To my gang, Anna Beranek, Atefa Parsa and Roberto Hortas, Rebecca McClure, Katrine Thue and Sebastian Cohnen, your loyalty is unparalleled. To 'the coven', Michelle McKenzie, Daniela Exley, and especially

Simone Smith who keeps me grounded when I feel lost. My 'good vibes crew', Birgit Ströbel, Maike Buhr, Maria Jose Perea Marquez and Nathalie Fabre, thank you for the beautiful years of goal setting and pep talks. My book mastermind duo, Alan Newton and Nils Boeffel, thank you for the accountability nudges, and my personal photographer, Maren Richter, for, quite literally, making me look good.

A sincere thank you to all the friends around the world who contributed to my understanding of what individual leadership and courage entails. Much gratitude to my mentors, Jackie Kinsey, Burju Erdem and Andrea Claussen; dear friends Anette Maier, Caroline Morisette, Simona Cara and the core MBA reunion crew, and social advocates extraordinaire, Els Van Langenhove, Virginie Odinet, Giulia Guicciardini and Julia Bouric. And to Daniele Farinaccia and Josie Consiglio, the original social leaders; you led with care and inspired me every day, thank you.

To the early readers and experts who stress-tested these ideas before they reached the page: I am deeply grateful for your time, honesty and belief. To the TinyBox Academy audience members, workshop participants and clients who shared their stories and helped me shape the Social Leadership framework; you are the reason this work exists.

To the Mayfly Maven and Wayfinders Summit community, who inspire and humble me daily with your resilience, courage and power, thank you for trusting me with your voices. And finally, to my Rethink Press publishing team, led by Eve Makepeace, you put this book in my hands. Let's do it again soon.

Nothing meaningful happens in isolation. *Every Voice Matters*, and this book simply would not exist without yours.

Notes

1 A 'killer profile' is a clear, compelling and credible profile that instantly shows who you are, what you do and why you're valuable, so the right people want to connect and work with you.
2 World Health Organization, 'Coronavirus disease (COVID-19)' (WHO), www.who.int/health-topics/coronavirus#tab=tab_1, accessed 15 November 2025
3 'Cancel culture' is the practice of publicly shaming and boycotting a person or organisation, usually online, after they're seen to have done something offensive or unacceptable.
4 J Koblin, 'CBS Canceling 'Late Show With Stephen Colbert' After Next Season', *New York Times* (17 July 2025), www.nytimes.com/2025/07/17/business/stephen-colbert-late-show-ending.html, accessed 15 November 2025
5 Z Sharf, 'Jennifer Aniston says Disney+ and Hulu cancellations 'spoke volumes' after Jimmy Kimmel's suspension: That was 'dangerous' and 'unthinkable'' (Variety, 2025), https://variety.com/2025/tv/news/jennifer-aniston-jimmy-kimmel-suspension-dangerous-1236579731, accessed 15 November 2025

6 S Covey, *The 7 Habits of Highly Effective People* (Simon & Schuster in partnership with Franklin Covey, 2020)

7 United States Department of Justice Civil Rights Division and United States Attorney's Office District of Minnesota Civil Division, *Investigation of the City of Minneapolis and the Minneapolis Police Department, June 16, 2023* (US Justice System Report, 2023), www.justice.gov/d9/2023-06/minneapolis_findings_report.pdf, accessed 15 November 2025

8 L Asmelash, 'How Black Lives Matter went from a hashtag to a global rallying cry' (CNN, 26 July 2020), https://edition.cnn.com/2020/07/26/us/black-lives-matter-explainer-trnd, accessed 15 November 2025

9 NAACP, The 1963 March on Washington: A quarter million people and a dream (NAACP, 2020), https://naacp.org/find-resources/history-explained/1963-march-washington, accessed 15 November 2025

10 'Fake news' is false or misleading information that is presented as real news, often to manipulate opinions, provoke reactions, or generate clicks.

11 TEDx is a grassroots initiative bringing the spirit of TED to local communities around the globe: www.ted.com/about/programs-initiatives/tedx-program, accessed 15 November 2025

12 R Hayer, 'Addicted to AI: A patient's perspective on big data and technology' (25 May 2021), https://youtu.be/aKMcPtmrYFU?si=cq-0R00fA4dBzrQv, accessed 15 November 2025

13 M Gawdat, *Scary Smart: The future of Artificial Intelligence and how you can save our world* (Bluebird, 2021)

14 Blockchain technology is a digital system for recording transactions in a secure, transparent and tamper-resistant way, using a shared ledger that is stored and verified across many computers rather than one central server.

15 Nostr is an open, decentralised social networking protocol that lets people post and follow content without relying on a single company or platform.

16 Myers-Briggs (MBTI) is a personality assessment that sorts people into 16 types based on how they prefer to get energy (introvert/extrovert), take in information, make decisions and organise their world: www.myersbriggs.org, accessed 15 November 2025

17 16Personalities.com offers a popular free personality test, inspired by the Myers-Briggs framework: www.16personalities.com, accessed 15 November 2025
18 MotivStrukturAnalyse (MSA®) is a German personality assessment that measures 18 core motives to reveal a person's inner drivers, and is used in coaching, leadership development, team building and personal growth: https://msaprofil.com, accessed 15 November 2025
19 Edelman Trust Institute, *2025 Edelman Trust Barometer Global Report* (Edelman Trust Institute, 2025), www.edelman.com/sites/g/files/aatuss191/files/2025-01/2025%20Edelman%20Trust%20Barometer_Final.pdf, accessed 15 November 2025
20 Edelman Trust Institute, *2022 Edelman Trust Barometer Global Report* (Edelman Trust Institute, 2022), www.edelman.com/trust/2022-trust-barometer, accessed 15 November 2025
21 P Cohen, 'One Company's New Minimum Wage: $70,000 a Year', *New York Times* (14 April 2025), www.nytimes.com/2015/04/14/business/owner-of-gravity-payments-a-credit-card-processor-is-setting-a-new-minimum-wage-70000-a-year.html, accessed 15 November 2025
22 N Kristof, 'The $70,000-a-Year Minimum Wage', *New York Times* (30 March 2019), www.nytimes.com/2019/03/30/opinion/sunday/dan-price-minimum-wage.html, accessed 15 November 2025
23 Ibid
24 R Hayer, interview with Jürgen Schmitt (2021), unpublished
25 B Levitt, 'The true story behind *Swiped*, Whitney Wolfe Herd, and the birth of Bumble', *Time* (19 September 2025), https://time.com/7314564/swiped-true-story-whitney-wolfe-herd-bumble, accessed 15 November 2025
26 Habitat for Humanity, www.habitat.org, accessed 15 November 2025
27 Values comparison table adapted from Brigit Ströbel, with permission. Ströbel Business Empowerment, www.linkedin.com/in/birgitstroebel
28 LinkedIn Profile 2025, www.linkedin.com/in/aneeshraman, accessed 15 November 2025
29 J Ma, 'AI is 'breaking' entry-level jobs that Gen Z workers need to launch careers, LinkedIn exec warns' (*Fortune*, 25

May 2025), https://fortune.com/2025/05/25/ai-entry-level-jobs-gen-z-careers-young-workers-linkedin, accessed 15 November 2025

30 M Kinder, 'Hollywood writers went on strike to protect their livelihoods from generative AI. Their remarkable victory matters for all workers' (Brookings, 2024), www.brookings.edu/articles/hollywood-writers-went-on-strike-to-protect-their-livelihoods-from-generative-ai-their-remarkable-victory-matters-for-all-workers, accessed 15 November 2025

31 ITV News, 'HSBC resolves online banking and app outage after thousands of customers locked out of accounts' (ITV, 27 August 2025), www.itv.com/news/2025-08-27/hsbc-investigating-after-customers-unable-to-access-online-banking-and-app, accessed 15 November 2025

32 N Quinn, LinkedIn post (LinkedIn, 2020), www.linkedin.com/posts/noel-quinn-hsbc_hi-all-this-is-my-first-post-on-linkedin-activity-6718855172312985601-G4Fv?utm_source=social_share_send&utm_medium=member_desktop_web&rcm=ACoAAAEcQNsBqBpyesXCsPE7DV74mdrEHD4FR64, accessed 15 November 2025

33 V Giang, 'Here's Why People Started Hammering Fridges Outside Siemens' Beijing Headquarters' (Business Insider, 24 November 2011), www.businessinsider.com/siemens-fridge-doors-2011-11, accessed 27 January 2026

34 2022 Edelman Trust Barometer Global Report (Edelman Trust Institute, 2022), www.edelman.com/trust/2022-trust-barometer, accessed 15 November 2025

35 3DEXCITE, 'Sustainable Consumption: Avoid greenwashing and green hushing with digital authenticity' (2023), www.youtube.com/watch?v=Z12OjrPx31Q&list=PL3DN7eYIDW_Cg8_QUNhMStU8bUMRp_qvV&index=5, accessed 17 November 2025

36 B Corp certification is a designation awarded by the non-profit organisation B Lab to companies that meet high standards of social and environmental performance, transparency and accountability.

37 Cabaïa, 'Endowment Fund' (Cabaïa, 2025), www.cabaia.com/pages/endowment-fund?utm_source=chatgpt.com, accessed 16 November 2025

38 Cabaïa, 'Wings of the Ocean' (Cabaïa, 2025), www.cabaia.com/de-de/collections/partnerschaft-wings-of-the-ocean, accessed 16 November 2025

39 Cabaïa, 'Our Commitments' (Cabaïa, 2025), www.cabaia.com/en-de/pages/environment, accessed 16 November 2025
40 A Sivasankar, 'Grameen Bank: The microfinance revolution and its role in women empowerment' (Centre For Development Policy And Practice, 2024), www.cdpp.co.in/articles/grameen-bank-the-microfinance-revolution-and-its-role-in-women-empowerment, accessed 15 November 2025
41 TOMS, 'Our Story: Better tomorrows begin with TOMS' (TOMS website), www.toms.com/en-us/about-toms, accessed 16 November 2025
42 Patagonia, 'Our environmental impact programs' (Patagonia website), www.patagonia.com/our-responsibility-programs.html, accessed 16 November 2025
43 S Barr, 'Olympic athlete Allyson Felix says Nike wanted to pay her 70% less after giving birth', *The Independent* (23 May 2019), www.independent.co.uk/life-style/health-and-families/allyson-felix-olympic-athlete-sprinter-nike-give-birth-mother-contract-a8926611.html, accessed 16 November 2025
44 M Walker-Khan, 'Allyson Felix: Five reasons the sprinter will forever be a legend' (BBC Sports, 16 July 2022), www.bbc.com/sport/athletics/62169873, accessed 16 November 2025
45 Department of Economic and Social Affairs: Sustainable Development, Secretary-General Mr Kofi Annan (United Nations, 2024), https://sdgs.un.org/statements/secretary-general-mr-kofi-annan-9512, accessed 16 November 2025
46 Department of Economic and Social Affairs: Sustainable Development, The 17 Goals (United Nations, 2016), https://sdgs.un.org/goals, accessed 16 November 2025
47 Hope Platform, https://findhope.io
48 Young Minds UK, www.youngminds.org.uk
49 TinyBox Academy, www.tinybox.academy/workshops
50 Mayfly Maven, www.mayflymaven.com
51 EU Business School Munich, www.euruni.edu/en/Campuses/Munich.html
52 The Wayfinders Summit, https://wayfinderssummit.com
53 Dassault Systèmes, Women in technology (Dassault Systèmes, 2019), www.3ds.com/insights/corporate-reports/women-technology, accessed 17 November 2025

54 J Williams, 'Malala Yousafzai and the BBC' (BBC News, 19 October 2012), www.bbc.co.uk/blogs/theeditors/2012/10/malala_yousafzai_and_the_bbc.html, accessed 15 November 2025
55 Malala Fund, https://malala.org/about, accessed 15 November 2025
56 Prize announcement 2014 (The Nobel Prize, 2014), www.nobelprize.org/prizes/peace/2014/prize-announcement, accessed 15 November 2025
57 M Igini, 'Fridays for Future: How young climate activists are making their voices heard (Earth Org, 2022), https://earth.org/fridays-for-future, accessed 15 November 2025
58 K Hasegawa, 'Fridays for Future: A social movements perspective' (Global Dialogue, 2022), https://globaldialogue.isa-sociology.org/articles/fridays-for-future-a-social-movements-perspective, accessed 15 November 2025
59 S Chan, 'Financial crisis was avoidable, inquiry finds', *New York Times* (26 January 2011), www.nytimes.com/2011/01/26/business/economy/26inquiry.html, accessed 15 November 2025
60 TD Bank, 'Investor relations' (TD Bank website), www.td.com/ca/en/about-td/for-investors/investor-relations/share-information/share-price-tools/historical-lookup-price, accessed 15 November 2025
61 L Huang, Leading the Nation through Social Media: Jacinda Ardern's Self-presentation on Facebook during the Covid-19 Crisis (Auckland University of Technology, 2021), https://openrepository.aut.ac.nz/server/api/core/bitstreams/c3477a8d-fabf-4302-8a53-ac7dba4bd441/content, accessed 15 November 2025
62 KB Monin, 'Framing and agenda setting following the mass shooting terror attack in Christchurch (University of Chicago, 2023), https://crownschool.uchicago.edu/student-life/advocates-forum/framing-and-agenda-setting-following-mass-shooting-terror-attack, accessed 15 November 2025
63 Harvard School of Public Health, 'How Jacinda Ardern tackled public health crises in New Zealand' (Harvard TH Chan, 2023), https://hsph.harvard.edu/news/how-jacinda-ardern-tackled-public-health-crises-in-new-zealand, accessed 15 November 2025

64 A Connolly, 'Understanding employee turnover statistics and trends for 2024' (Hubstaff Blog 2024), https://hubstaff.com/blog/employee-turnover-statistics, accessed 15 November 2025
65 S Sinek, 'Start With Why: How great leaders inspire action' (TEDxPugetSound, 2009), https://youtu.be/u4ZoJKF_VuA?si=Qfzd_ZshIVtDyqn9, accessed 15 November 2025
66 Lynchy, 'Australian campaigns of the decade: Coca-Cola 'Share a Coke' (2011) via Ogilvy Sydney' (Campaign Brief, 2019), https://campaignbrief.com/australian-campaigns-of-the-decade%E2%80%88coca-cola-share-a-coke-2011-via-ogilvy-sydney, accessed 15 November 2025
67 J Walfisz, 'Eminem loses five-year legal battle with Spotify over music streaming rights' (Euronews, 2024), www.euronews.com/culture/2024/09/05/eminem-loses-five-year-legal-battle-with-spotify-over-music-streaming-rights, accessed 15 November 2025
68 TrueLoyal, '8 brands who nailed user-generated content marketing' (TrueLoyal, 2019), www.trueloyal.com/blog/8-brands-nailed-user-generated-content-marketing, accessed 15 November 2025
69 N Bojkov, '21 user-generated content examples for your next marketing campaign' (Embed Social, 2025), https://embedsocial.com/blog/user-generated-content-examples, accessed 15 November 2025
70 C Tams, 'The co-creation imperative: How to make organizational change collaborative' (*Forbes*, 2018), www.forbes.com/sites/carstentams/2018/02/11/the-co-creation-imperative-how-to-make-organizational-change-collaborative, accessed 15 November 2025
71 First Round, 'How Notion does marketing: A deep-dive into its community, influencers and growth playbooks, (First Round, 2024), https://review.firstround.com/how-notion-does-marketing-a-deep-dive-into-its-community-influencers-growth-playbooks, accessed 15 November 2025
72 People Analytics World (previously Tucana Global Conference), https://peopleanalyticsworld.com, accessed 16 November 2025
73 B Hogan, 'How Dropbox's people-first culture fosters connection and growth' (Built in San Francisco, 2023), www.builtinsf.com/articles/how-dropboxs-people-first-culture-fosters-connection-and-growth, accessed 16 November 2025

74 H Friedl, LinkedIn profile Harald Friedl (LinkedIn, 2025), www.linkedin.com/in/harald-friedl, accessed 16 November 2025
75 www.haraldfriedl.earth, accessed 16 November 2025
76 B Gallegos, '9 B2B social media examples to inspire your strategy' (Everyone Social, 2024), https://everyonesocial.com/blog/b2b-social-media-examples, accessed 16 November 2025
77 J Liu, LinkedIn profile Jingjin Liu, www.linkedin.com/in/jingjin-liu, accessed 16 November 2025
78 T Warren, 'Zoom grows to 300 million meeting participants despite security backlash' (The Verge, 2020), www.theverge.com/2020/4/23/21232401/zoom-300-million-users-growth-coronavirus-pandemic-security-privacy-concerns-response, accessed 16 November 2025
79 D Diamond, 'The ALS Ice Bucket Challenge has raised $100 million – and counting' (*Forbes*, 29 August 2014), www.forbes.com/sites/dandiamond/2014/08/29/the-als-ice-bucket-challenge-has-raised-100m-but-its-finally-cooling-off, accessed 15 November 2025
80 ALS Association, 'ALS Ice Bucket Challenge year-end update' (ALS, 30 January 2018), www.als.org/blog/als-ice-bucket-challenge-year-end-update-over-94-million-commitments-2014, accessed 15 November 2025
81 K Camero, 'A decade later: How the ALS Ice Bucket Challenge made a lasting impact' (National Geographic, 2023), www.nationalgeographic.com/science/article/als-ice-bucket-challenge-research-impact, accessed 15 November 2025
82 MUSC News, 'Simone Biles can be mental health role model, psychiatrist says' (MUSC, 2021), https://web.musc.edu/about/news-center/2021/07/30/simone-biles-can-be-mental-health-role-model-psychiatrist-says, accessed 18 November 2025
83 Olympics, 'Simone Biles: All titles, records and medals – complete list' (Olympics, 2024), www.olympics.com/en/news/simone-biles-all-titles-records-and-medals-complete-list-paris-2024, accessed 18 November 2025
84 M Schaefer, *The Greatest Marketing Book Ever* (Schaefer Marketing Solutions, 2023)
85 F Christopher, 'How did Mr Beast get so popular?' (Medium, 2024), https://medium.com/faunce/how-did-mr-beast-become-so-popular-3887ab3e1f35, accessed 16 November 2025

86 H Lux, 'Disney fined a PTA for showing *The Lion King* at a fundraising event to benefit students' (Upworthy, 2020), www.upworthy.com/disney-fined-school-lion-king, accessed 16 November 2025

87 'Viral' or 'going viral' is when a piece of content spreads extremely quickly and widely online, reaching a huge audience in a short period of time through rapid sharing.

88 LR France, 'Will Smith issues apology to Chris Rock over slapping incident at Oscars' (CNN, 2022), https://edition.cnn.com/2022/03/28/entertainment/will-smith-apology/index.html, accessed 16 November 2025

89 W Smith, Instagram post apologising to Chris Rock after the Oscars incident (Instagram, 2022), www.instagram.com/p/CbqmaY1p7Pz, accessed 16 November 2025

90 SurveySparrow, 'What is customer service? The complete guide with strategies for 2025' (SparrowDesk, 2025), www.sparrowdesk.com/blogs/customer-service-guide, accessed 16 November 2025

91 C O'Brien, 'What Hootsuite founder Ryan Holmes learned from his own social media fail: "Own it. Apologize"' (VentureBeat, 2017), https://venturebeat.com/ai/what-hootsuite-founder-ryan-holmes-learned-from-his-own-social-media-fail-own-it-apologize, accessed 16 November 2025

92 BBC, '#BBCtrending: Did Between Two Ferns really help Obamacare?' (BBC News, 2014), www.bbc.com/news/entertainment-arts-26526620, accessed 15 November 2025

93 S Cain, 'Lizzo removes "harmful" lyric in new song Grrrls after ableism criticism', (*The Guardian*, 14 June 2022), www.theguardian.com/music/2022/jun/14/lizzo-removes-harmful-ableist-slur-from-new-song-grrrls-after-criticism, accessed 18 November 2025

94 A Bailey, 'Emma Watson on how the criticism of her activism affected her' (*Elle*, 14 February 2017), www.elle.com/culture/celebrities/news/a43044/emma-watson-on-feminist-criticism-elle-uk-march-2017-interview, accessed 16 November 2025

95 'Struggle porn' describes the glorification of overwork and perpetual hustle as something to brag about and admire, rather than a sign that something is out of balance.

96 C Beale, 'Is Gary Vaynerchuk "wrong, wrong, wrong, wrong, wrong" about media?' (Campaign, 2019),

www.campaignlive.co.uk/article/gary-vaynerchuk-wrong-wrong-wrong-wrong-wrong-media/1663992, accessed 16 November 2025
97 A Magati wallet uses NFC/RFID blockers for maximum protection and integrates the Apple AirTag.
98 C Price, *How to Break Up with Your Phone*, revised edition (Penguin Random House, 2025)
99 Royal Society for Public Health, '#StatusOfMind: Social media and young people's mental health and wellbeing' (RSPH, 2017), www.rsph.org.uk/our-work/campaigns/status-of-mind.html, accessed 18 November 2025
100 Internet Live Stats, 'Twitter usage statistics' (Internet Live Stats, 2013–2025), www.internetlivestats.com/twitter-statistics, accessed 16 November 2025
101 T Oladipo, *'31 TikTok Statistics to Know in 2025'* (Buffer, 2025), https://buffer.com/resources/tiktok-statistics, accessed 16 November 2025
102 Metricool, *'Instagram statistics in 2025 every marketer should know'* (Metricool, 2025), https://metricool.com/important-instagram-statistics, accessed 16 November 2025
103 A Parmar, 'How I gained 67,000 followers on Medium in under 3 years' (The BAE HQ), www.thebaehq.com/stories/how-i-gained-67-000-followers-on-medium-in-under-3-years, accessed 18 November 2025
104 Shopify Growth Centre, '23 Shopify success stories to share with your audience' (Shopify, 2025), https://growthcenter.shopify.com/blogs/shopify-101/23-shopify-success-stories-to-share-with-your-audience, accessed 16 November 2025
105 R Aman, 'Jessica Alba: The quintessential Hollywood star and entrepreneurial visionary' (Vocal Media, 2025), https://vocal.media/motivation/jessica-alba-the-quintessential-hollywood-star-and-entrepreneurial-visionary, accessed 16 November 2025
106 SIM Joel, 'The Honest Company: What entrepreneurs can learn from this natural baby and beauty company' (Capitalism, 2023), www.capitalism.com/the-honest-company, accessed 16 November 2025
107 R Hayer, 'Addicted to AI: A patient's perspective on Big Data and technology | Raj Hayer | TEDxUWMilwaukee' (25 May 2021), www.youtube.com/watch?v=aKMcPtmrYFU, accessed 30 December 2025

108 C Gallo, 'Richard Branson on storytelling that sparks ideas and builds brands' (*Forbes*, 2017), www.forbes.com/sites/carminegallo/2017/03/24/richard-branson-on-storytelling-that-sparks-ideas-and-build-brands, accessed 16 November 2025

109 S Sinek, 'Start with Why: How great leaders inspire action | Simon Sinek | TEDxPugetSound' (29 September 2009), www.youtube.com/watch?v=u4ZoJKF_VuA, accessed 30 December 2025

110 L Gallagher, 'The inside story behind the unlikely rise of Airbnb' (Knowledge@Wharton, 2017), https://knowledge.wharton.upenn.edu/podcast/knowledge-at-wharton-podcast/the-inside-story-behind-the-unlikely-rise-of-airbnb, accessed 16 November 2025

111 B Brown, 'The power of vulnerability' (TEDxHouston, 2010), www.ted.com/talks/brene_brown_the_power_of_vulnerability, accessed 16 November 2025

112 A De Mello, *Awareness: The perils and opportunities of reality* (Image, 1990)

113 S Krawcheck, LinkedIn Profile Sallie Krawcheck (LinkedIn), www.linkedin.com/in/salliekrawcheck, accessed 16 November 2025

114 J D'Onfro, 'The truth about Google's famous "20% time" policy' (Business Insider, 2015), www.businessinsider.com/google-20-percent-time-policy-2015-4, accessed 17 November 2025

115 Econsultancy, 'How Glossier has used Instagram to create a cult following' (Econsultancy, 2016), https://econsultancy.com/how-glossier-has-used-instagram-to-create-a-cult-following, accessed 16 November 2025

116 The Fashion Law, *'Glossier raises $80 million in latest round, valuing the beauty brand at 5.8 billion'* (The Fashion Law, 2021), www.thefashionlaw.com/glossier-raises-80-million-in-latest-round-valuing-the-beauty-brand-at-1-8-billion, accessed 16 November 2025

117 K Yu, 'It's the RED CUPS season! Check out how this brand has been dominating the holidays since 1997' (Valens Research, 2021), www.valens-research.com/dynamic-marketing-communique/its-the-red-cups-season-check-out-how-this-brand-has-been-dominating-the-holidays-since-1997-fridays-gorillas-of-guerrilla-marketing, accessed 16 November 2025

118 NACS, 'Starbucks draws in customers with red cup' (NACS Daily, 2024), www.convenience.org/Media/Daily/2024/December/4/3-Starbucks-Draws-Customers-With-Red-Cup_Research, accessed 16 November 2025

119 Credit Suisse Research Institute, *The CS Gender 3000: The reward for change* (Credit Suisse, 2017), https://evolveetfs.com/wp-content/uploads/2017/08/Credit-Suisse-Reward-for-Change_1495660293279_2.pdf, accessed 19 November 2025

120 Boston Consulting Group, *How Diverse Leadership Teams Boost Innovation* (BCG, 2018), https://web-assets.bcg.com/img-src/BCG-How-Diverse-Leadership-Teams-Boost-Innovation-Jan-2018_tcm9-207935.pdf, accessed 19 November 2025

121 The Global Executive MBA is an advanced master's business degree designed for experienced and mid-to-senior leaders at St Gallen University, taught across multiple countries and campuses.

122 The Project Management Professional (PMP) is a globally recognised certification from the Project Management Institute (PMI).

123 K Crenshaw, 'Kimberlé Crenshaw on intersectionality, more than two decades later' (Columbia Law School, 2017), www.law.columbia.edu/news/archive/kimberle-crenshaw-intersectionality-more-two-decades-later, accessed 16 November 2025

124 A Fennell, 'Candidate experience statistics 2025' (StandOut CV, 2025), https://standout-cv.com/stats/candidate-experience-statistics, accessed 16 November 2025

125 First Page Sage, Average Customer Acquisition Cost (CAC) in Banking (First Page Sage, 2024), https://firstpagesage.com/seo-blog/average-customer-acquisition-cost-cac-in-banking, accessed 16 November 2025

126 Ibid

127 D Bose et al, 'Vulnerability of female drivers involved in motor vehicle crashes' (AAAM, 2011), www.ncbi.nlm.nih.gov/pmc/articles/PMC3222446, accessed 16 November 2025

128 US Global Investors, 'How M-PESA is leading a financial revolution across Africa' (US Global Investors, 2024), www.usfunds.com/resource/how-m-pesa-is-leading-a-financial-revolution-across-africa, accessed 16 November 2025

129 MSCI, *Corporate Responsibility* (MSCI), www.msci.com/discover-msci/corporate-responsibility, accessed 16 November 2025
130 S Dixon-Fyle, K Dolan, V Hunt and S Prince, '*Diversity wins: How inclusion matters*' (McKinsey & Company, 2020), www.mckinsey.com/featured-insights/diversity-and-inclusion/diversity-wins-how-inclusion-matters, accessed 16 November 2025
131 SE Garcia, 'The woman who created #MeToo long before hashtags', *The New York Times* (20 October 2017), www.nytimes.com/2017/10/20/us/me-too-movement-tarana-burke.html, accessed 16 November 2025
132 Global Fund for Women, 'What is the 'Me Too' movement?' (Global Fund for Women), www.globalfundforwomen.org/movements/me-too, accessed 16 November 2025
133 A Gliadkovskaya, 'Melinda French Gates announces $250M fund to improve women's health' (Fierce Healthcare, 2024), www.fiercehealthcare.com/finance/melinda-french-gates-announces-250m-fund-improve-womens-health, accessed 16 November 2025

Recommended Reading

Bourke, Juliet and Dillon, Bernadette, 'The diversity and inclusion revolution: Eight powerful truths' (Deloitte, January 2018), https://internationalwim.org/wp-content/uploads/2020/12/Deloitte-DI-2019.pdf – a concise, practical summary of what moves the needle on D&I in organisations.

Burkeman, Oliver, *Four Thousand Weeks: Time management for mortals* (Vintage, 2022) – an honest, big-picture look at time, limits and what matters, perfect for rethinking productivity and 'busy' culture.

Cameron, Julia, *The Artist's Way: A spiritual path to higher creativity* (Souvenir Press, 2020) – a classic twelve-week toolkit for unblocking creativity and recovering your voice through simple, consistent practices.

Carnegie, Dale, *How to Win Friends and Influence People* (Vermillion, 2006) – timeless principles for building trust, handling conflict, and positively influencing others.

Covey, Stephen R, *The 7 Habits of Highly Effective People: 30*th *anniversary edition* (Simon & Schuster UK, 2020) – a foundational framework for personal leadership that underpins modern thinking on habits and character.

Crawford, Kate, *Atlas of AI: Power, politics and the planetary costs of artificial intelligence* (Yale University Press, 2021) – a powerful look at the human, environmental and political costs of AI, essential if you care about responsible, human-centred technology.

Credit Suisse Research Institute, *The CS Gender 3000: The reward for change* (Credit Suisse, September 2016), https://evolveetfs.com/wp-content/uploads/2017/08/Credit-Suisse-Reward-for-Change_1495660293279_2.pdf – financial analysis connecting gender-diverse leadership with company performance.

Dicks, Matthew, *Storyworthy: Engage, teach, persuade and change your life through the power of storytelling* (New World Library, 2018) – a practical, funny guide to turning real-life moments into compelling stories you can use in talks, books and conversations.

Fitzpatrick, Rob, *Write Useful Books: A modern approach to designing and refining recommendable non-fiction* (Useful Books Ltd, 2021) – a practical playbook for non-fiction writing that solves readers' problems and sells over the long-term.

Gawdat, Mo, *Scary Smart: The future of artificial intelligence and how you can save our world* (Bluebird, 2022) – an urgent look at how AI is evolving, why our choices right now matter and how to shape technology with ethics, compassion and human-centred values.

Guenole, Nigel, Ferrar, Jonathan and Feinzig, Sheri, *The Power of People* (Pearson FT Press, 2017) – a practical guide to using people analytics to build better workplaces, decisions and cultures.

Kaplan, Mark and Donovan, Mason, *The Inclusion Dividend: Why investing in diversity & inclusion pays off* (DG Press, 2019) – a clear business case and roadmap for embedding inclusion into daily leadership and seeing concrete returns.

Kleon, Austin, *Keep Going: 10 ways to stay creative in good times and bad* (Workman Adult, 2019) – bite-sized, honest encouragement to keep making and sharing your work, especially when life feels chaotic or progress feels slow.

Lorenzo, Rocio, Voight, Nicole, Tsusaka, Miki, Krentz, Matt and Abouzahr, Katie, *How Diverse*

Leadership Teams Boost Innovation (Boston Consulting Group, 23 January 2018), www.bcg.com/publications/2018/how-diverse-leadership-teams-boost-innovation – evidence that diversity at the top directly links to higher innovation revenue.

McKinsey & Company, *Diversity Wins: How inclusion matters* (McKinsey & Company, May 2020), www.mckinsey.com/~/media/mckinsey/featured%20insights/diversity%20and%20inclusion/diversity%20wins%20how%20inclusion%20matters/diversity-wins-how-inclusion-matters-vf.pdf – compelling global data showing how diverse, inclusive organisations outperform.

Nestor, James, *Breath* (Penguin Life, 2021) – a fascinating exploration of how something as simple as how we breathe affects our health, focus and performance.

Pink, Daniel H, *Drive: The surprising truth about what motivates us* (Canongate Books, 2018) – a smart look at what really motivates us beyond carrots and sticks, essential for designing great work, teams and goals.

Ruiz, Don Miguel, *The Four Agreements* (Amber-Allen Publishing, 2018) – a simple framework for living and leading with integrity and clarity.

Sinek, Simon, *Start With Why: How great leaders inspire everyone to take action* (Penguin, 2011) – a foundational read on purpose-led leadership and communication, showing how clear 'why' creates trust, loyalty and momentum.

Thaler, Richard H and Sunstein, Cass R, *Nudge: The final edition* (Penguin, 2022) – how small changes in choice architecture shape behaviour, for anyone influencing decisions, products or policy.

Vallor, Shannon, *The AI Mirror: How to Reclaim Our Humanity in an Age of Machine Thinking* (OUP, USA, 2024) – a thoughtful guide to how AI reflects and reshapes our values, and what it means to stay fully human in a machine-shaped world.

Voss, Chris, *Never Split the Difference: Negotiating as if your life depended on it* (Random House Business, 2017) – high-stakes negotiation lessons from an ex-FBI hostage negotiator, translated into everyday conversations and difficult discussions.

The Author

Raj Hayer is a multi-award-winning CEO and founder of TinyBox Academy and Mayfly Maven, award-winning strategy expert, coach and motivational speaker. Crowned 'Best CEO in the Event Management Industry' and 'Best Corporate Learning Culture Innovator' by Business Worldwide Magazine, her work has appeared in *Authority Magazine, The Telegraph, Thrive, Business News Today, Passion Vista, Global Tech Times* and more.

She is regularly requested by leading organisations including Dassault Systèmes, Google Cloud and Siemens AG to speak about Social Leadership, business strategy and the power of influence and diversity. Her hugely popular TEDx Talk 'Addicted to AI: A patient's perspective on Big Data and technology' has garnered thousands of views and she is featured on the global International Women's Day speaker list.

When Raj is not on stage, she creates and delivers transformative events for international brands including PUMA and bespoke programmes for C-level executives. She lives between Munich and London but is always eager to retreat to remote locales for inspiration.

www.rajhayer.com/book

www.linkedin.com/in/rajhayer

TINYBOX

TinyBox Academy is a global training and event experience company for international brands including PUMA, Dassault Systèmes and Google Cloud. The Future-Ready Culture Lab delivers workshops that drive cultural transformation and prepare teams to drive innovation through AI adoption and tech readiness.

www.tinybox.academy

www.linkedin.com/company/tinyboxacademy

Mayfly Maven is an expert community that delivers transformative experiences for ambitious female leaders and entrepreneurs. Through education, coaching and in-person events, the community supports women to amplify their voice, story, power and wealth.

www.mayflymaven.com

www.linkedin.com/company/mayfly-maven

www.ingramcontent.com/pod-product-compliance
Lightning Source LLC
LaVergne TN
LVHW030919080826
845145LV00013B/2960

* 9 7 8 1 7 8 1 3 3 9 7 6 3 *